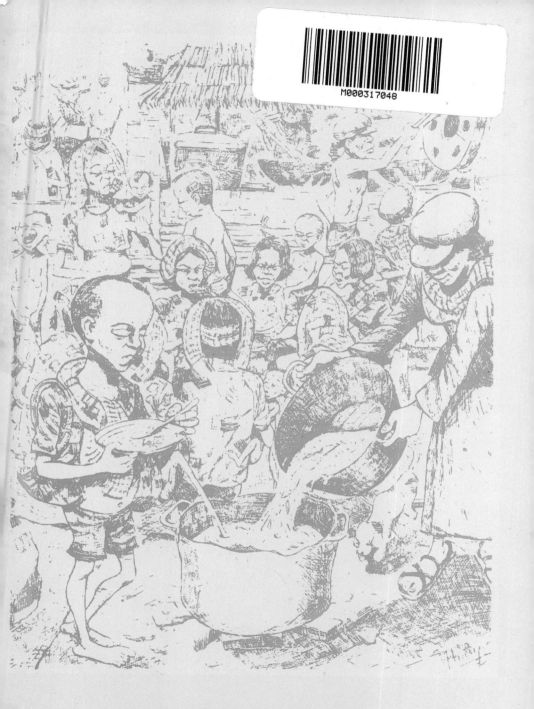

Communal dining first established outdoors.

the MURDEROUS REVOLUTION

ASIAN
PORTRAITS

VISAGE
D'ASIE

THE MURDEROUS REVOLUTION

LIFE AND DEATH IN POL POT'S KAMPUCHEA

Martin Stuart-Fox
Bunheang Ung

Orchid Press
Bangkok 1998

Martin Stuart-Fox
Bunheang Ung
THE MURDEROUS REVOLUTION
LIFE AND DEATH IN POL POT'S KAMPUCHEA

First published 1985 in Australia
Reprinted 1986,1998

Published by
Orchid Press
98/13 Soi Apha Phirom, Ratchada Road
Chatuchak, Bangkok 10900, Thailand

ISBN 974-8299-14-7

"Under Pol Pot, for three years, eight months, and twenty days, our people lived in hell"

--Keo Samuth[*]

This book is dedicated to the Kampuchean people, the living and the dead.

[*] in "Interviews in Kampuchea", *Bulletin of Concerned Scholars,* 14, No.4, 1982.

ACKNOWLEDGEMENT

We would like to acknowledge the help of a number of people who contributed in one way or another to the publication of this book. But to one person above all our thanks are due. Throughout those dark days in Kampuchea, and subsequently during the difficult period of resettlement in Australia, Phiny Ung was a constant source of encouragement and inspiration. These drawings and this book are hers too. Our thanks go also to Daniel Vevert who introduced us and suggested we work together, and to Kim Cheng Pich who ably assisted our mutual understanding. Ben Kiernan, Geoffrey Gunn and Carlyle Thayer kindly read the manuscript and offered many helpful suggestions. Mary Kooyman expertly did the typing, while Rod Bucknell cast a careful eye over the proofs. To all we offer our thanks.

Martin Stuart-Fox
Bunheang Ung

Preface to the first edition

For the outside world, the Kampuchean revolution was at first a mysterious happening that didn't concern anyone, and later a horrifying example of barbarity and the misuse of power from which all sorts of moral and political lessons could be drawn. Either way, it was remote and inexplicable. For the men, women and children who lived through it, however, it was a searing personal experience, just as inexplicable, but frighteningly and inescapably real. The survivors of the period of Khmer Rouge domination will carry the memory of those years for the rest of their lives. Few are the families which cannot count their dead: many saw children, or parents, or brothers, or sisters, die of malnutrition, disease, or outright starvation; some watched helplessly the arrest of close relatives or friends, knowing they would never see them again; some witnessed executions. None will forget the daily struggle to survive, the constant labour, the obsession with food, the fear of retribution for some minor or unknown crime.

Bunheang Ung has the visual memory of an artist. What remained etched on his mind was a series of indelible images: — the stunned disoriented mass of people evacuating the capital of Phnom Penh; the brutal arrogance of Khmer Rouge cadres; work with the Mobile Brigade of labourers of which he was a member; threshing rice; harvesting; attending "consciousness-building" seminars; the prison where his sisters-in-law died; the massacre of "new people"; and the bodies of the dead.

In Kampuchea, even after the Khmer Rouge regime had been overthrown by the Vietnamese, those images could not be given expression. Not until Bunheang and his family escaped to Thailand and came to Australia could he at last draw what continued to haunt his mind. For Bunheang the drawings reproduced in this book are both a record and a memorial: a record for the world, so that all may know of the sufferings of the Kampuchean people, and a memorial to those who have died. Drawing them was a kind of catharsis, an outpouring of pent-up emotions. Day after day with untiring compulsion he drew these stark images in Indian ink, with no colour, until the record was complete.

When I was shown the drawings by a mutual friend who suggested I might write a text to accompany them, and met Bun himself, I was struck by two things: the unique record that the drawings represented, and the intensity of the experiences that gave rise to them. No foreign or Kampuchean correspondents or photographers recorded the events of those years. The few publications of the regime were nothing more than propaganda — smiling peasants, rising production. When an occasional friendly news team was allowed to film in the country, as was a Yugoslav team, the visit was carefully controlled. The Yugoslavs were horrified at what they saw, but their film showed little of the misery of the people or the horror that later came to light. Bunheang's drawings thus represent an invaluable testimony to the brutal oppression of a regime whose utter contempt for human life can only be compared with those of Nazi Germany or the Soviet Union under Stalin.

During the many hours of interviews and conversations I had with Bunheang, I was impressed by the vividness of his memory, and the pain his experiences still caused him. The months and years of ceaseless labour were behind him, but his helplessness as his sisters-in-law were arrested, his revulsion as he realized the conditions under which they must have died, his horror when he witnessed assassinations in the Eastern Zone in 1978, all these were so real that he broke down in recounting them. What agony he felt as he drew those scenes, and relived them in his drawings, can only be imagined.

What Bunheang saw and experienced was but an isolated fragment of the national nightmare that was Kampuchea under the Khmer Rouge. It was impossible for him at the time to fit his own experiences into any overall pattern of events. Changes were ordered in the style of life, patterns of production and consumption, and even the relationships between individuals, for which no reasons were given. Nobody in his village of Maesor Prachan understood why new regulations were introduced, how decisions were arrived at, or what was happening at the national level. The secret workings of the Communist Party of Kampuchea (CPK) remained an enigma.

Since the overthrow of the Khmer Rouge regime, however, it has become possible to relate the personal experiences of individuals to the drama being played out at the centre of power in the CPK. Research by a small group of international scholars has enabled local events to be placed in a national perspective, one which not only explains something of what happened in the villages, but also provides a fascinating and horrifying glimpse of the thinking and actions of those involved in the struggle for power in the Party.

I have tried to describe both what happened to Bunheang as a person, and something of the background to the events he experienced. I have included not only an account of the rise of the Khmer Rouge (chapter 2) and of the power struggles and purges which tore the CPK apart (chapter 7), but I have also attempted to understand the thinking of that small group of ideologues who wielded such absolute power in Democratic Kampuchea (chapter 9). The view of the world which these men had, and their vision of the kind of Kampuchea they hoped to create, were largely responsible for the policy decisions of the regime.

These three background chapters could be omitted by those readers more interested in the personal drama of Bunheang Ung. So, too, the few numbered references in the text which refer to sources of information or additional readings can be ignored. All references are collected as end notes, which I trust will make the book of value to those students of contemporary Kampuchea who wish to probe more deeply into the recent history of this beautiful but unhappy land.

Martin Stuart-Fox
Brisbane August 1984

Preface to the third edition

Since the first edition of this book appeared in 1985 major developments have taken place both in Cambodia (as the country is now once again called) and in the region. ASEAN, the Association of Southeast Asian Nations, has expanded to include nine members, and would have welcomed Cambodia as its tenth had it not been for the political turmoil of mid-1997. As for Cambodia itself, the United Nations brokered peace agreement of 1991 at last offered hope of national reconciliation. Yet the deep wounds of war and revolution remain, and will take decades, rather than years, to heal.

I have outlined the recent history of Cambodia (for the fifteen years from 1982 to 1997) in a new Epilogue to this updated edition. I have also included a brief selected bibliography covering the growing body of research and writing on Cambodia and the Khmer Rouge that has appeared over this period. But the original edition of this book told much more than the story of the murderous revolution that wrecked Cambodia in the 1970s. It also told a personal story, the story of Phiny and Bunheang Ung and their struggle to survive.

So how have Bunheang and Phiny fared? When the family landed in Australia they brought with them their eldest daughter, Chan Kreusna, and Phiny was pregnant. Sita Nathalie was born in Brisbane while Bunheang was exorcising his oppressive memories through the drawings that illustrate this book. Ten years later Jesse Bunnawadh was born, and Justin Waddhana followed in 1993. By this time the family had moved to Sydney where Bunheang found work as a film cartoonist. Among the feature length cartoon films on which he worked was the Epic of Gilgamesh, the story of an ancient Mesopotamian hero ordered by the Iraqi regime of Saddam Hussein. When the studio closed down in 1988, Phiny and Bunheang opened the Apsara Restaurant, the first up-market Cambodian restaurant in Sydney offering finely cooked and immaculately presented traditional Cambodian cuisine. Forced to close as a result of the recession of the early 1990s, Bunheang went back to drawing for feature cartoons, this time as a freelancer on contract. In 1997 he became a regular political cartoonist for the Far Eastern Economic Review. Meanwhile Phiny was employed as an Ethnic Communities Liaison Officer, first with the Health Department, then with the Police with the difficult task of mediating cultural misunderstanding. Their eldest children are now at university.

Such is a bald account of a young family settling successfully in a new country. But this tells nothing of the struggle to adapt to new ways; nor of the agony of watching events unfold in Cambodia, of fear for the welfare of relatives left behind, of the hope that some day it would be possible to return. For Phiny and Bunheang the reality of the past was brought jarringly home to them in a particularly confronting way when in 1984 they came face to face on a Sydney street with Eak, the former Khmer Rouge chief of their home village of Maesor Prachan (see page 42). Eak had been purged as village chief along with other cadres in September 1976 (page 82), but was allowed to continue living quietly in the village. He thus escaped the final ruthless purge of Eastern Zone cadres when all serving Khmer Rouge officials in Maesor Prachan had been massacred (page 139). Later Eak and his large family left Maesor Prachan and made their way to a refugee camp in Thailand, where all were eventually accepted for resettlement in Australia.

Phiny and Bunheang were outraged, and decided to reveal the man's background. They talked to the newspapers; they went on television. Later, when the whole question of war crimes was again making news they took part in a recorded confrontation with Eak. But as Eak had been purged early as a Khmer Rouge cadre, he could claim not to have taken part in any killings. Though he had been village chief when Phiny's father, along with many others, had been taken away and killed, the evidence against Eak was not strong enough under Australian law to force his deportation. So Eak remains in Sydney, the wealthy owner of a restaurant and several other businesses in suburban Cabramatta.

The press exposure that resulted from the "outing" of Eak made Phiny an obvious candidate for a documentary on the first return home of a Cambodian from Australia after Vietnamese troops withdrew and serious peace moves got underway in 1989. It was a deeply painful experience to return again to Maesor Prachan, to see where the little thatched house she and Bunheang had shared once stood (it had since been destroyed), to meet those who remembered her. Most of all that visit, too brief because of security concerns, vividly brought back the deaths of her father and sisters. Her family home was occupied by strangers: she had to request permission to enter, while the government official accompanying the TV crew watched her every move. She felt stifled, and was glad to return to Australia.

With the signing of the peace agreement in October 1991, Bunheang too returned to Cambodia. He thought perhaps it might be possible to set up a cartoon studio in Phnom Penh to train Cambodian cartoonists. But his visit was premature; conditions were still too fluid. In December 1993, after the UN organized elections, Bunheang went back again. This time he found power shared between former enemies, and Cambodia with two prime ministers. Corruption was rife. Bunheang knew that to set up a studio he would have to pay off both sides. Moreover cartoonists are dangerous men: he could himself become the target of either side.

Back in Australia, Phiny and Bunheang made up their minds to stay. But they continued to follow events in Cambodia. They were not pleased to see Sihanouk become king, for they held him responsible for much of the tragedy of contemporary Cambodia. They are republicans, and distrust Sihanouk. For a while former Finance Minister Sam Rainsy held out some hope that he might do for Cambodia what the leaders of modern Singapore have done for their country - put an end to corruption and create a prosperous society. But Sam Rainsy wields no power in the new Cambodia.

When at last in mid-1997 reports were received that Pol Pot had been arrested by his own former followers, Phiny and Bunheang were immediately sceptical. Television footage of Pol Pot's carefully staged show trial only confirmed their suspicions. Pol Pot was treated as a respected elderly leader, assisted to walk and helped into his car. But the victims of Khmer Rouge justice were never treated like that. Bunheang believes that Pol Pot was sacrificing himself so that the Khmer Rouge as a political movement could survive to play a role in the politics of the country. And for that Bunheang even accords him some grudging respect.

What Cambodia needs, both Phiny and Bunheang believe, is a strong, dedicated and principled leader capable of building a social democracy based on Buddhist compassion for the poor and downtrodden. In their view, Hun Sen and Sihanouk make two of a kind: devious, calculating and corrupt. Sihanouk only led the country to ruin, and Hun Sen, obsessed like Sihanouk with monopolizing power, will do the same. But Cambodians, Bunheang fears, have a "trashbin" approach to history: they throw the past away, and learn nothing. We can only hope that he is wrong.

If Cambodian politicians learn little from history, however, others learn more. Thanks to research by a devoted band of scholars, we know far more about the Cambodian revolution now than we did fifteen years ago. In the light of their findings, and of recent debates over the nature of the Khmer Rouge regime, I should perhaps briefly clarify my own view of the dynamics of the Khmer Rouge revolution. For reasons as much political as academic, Khmer Rouge motivation has been labelled racist and genocidal. Racist it undoubtedly was, though primarily in its view of the Khmer themselves. And genocidal it was too, but only in relation to the Vietnamese, whom the Khmer Rouge both hated and feared with paranoic intensity. Other races - the Cham, the Chinese - suffered terribly, but then so did the Khmer themselves, and for the same reasons: too many were labled enemies of the revolution who were unprepared to remake themselves, and Cambodian society, in the ideologically driven image demanded by the Khmer Rouge leadership. What the Khmer Rouge inflicted on the Cambodian people, of all races, was done in the name of a perverted Marxism. What caused the revolutionary movement to turn in upon itself was its racially inspired obsessive distrust and fear of the Vietnamese.

Despite knowing so much more now about the Khmer Rouge regime, I have left the text of this edition unchanged. For this was a personal story, of courage and survival, given artistic expression at a moment in time through the unique medium of Bunheang's bleakly honest cartoon style drawings. Drawings and text together, therefore, constitute an historical record that should not be tampered with. For the horror and inhumanity they reveal must never be forgotten, by the people of Cambodia or by the rest of the world.

Martin Stuart-Fox
Brisbane, September 1997

SELECT BIBLIOGRAPHY

Becker, Elizabeth, *When the War was Over*. New York; Simon and Schuster, 1986.

Boua, Chantou, David P. Chandler and Ben Kiernan, eds., *Pol Pot Plans the Future: Confidential Leadership Documents from Democratic Kampuchea, 1976-77*. New Haven; Yale University Press, 1988.

Chanda, Nayan, *Brother Enemy: The War after the War*. New York; Harcourt, Brace Jovanovich, 1986.

Chandler, David P., *The Tragedy of Cambodian History: Politics, War and Revolution Since 1945*. New Haven; Yale University Press, 1991.

Chandler, David P., *A History of Cambodia*. 2nd ed. Boulder; Westview, 1992.

Chandler, David P., *Brother Number One: A Political Biography of Pol Pot*. Boulder; Westview, 1992.

Chandler, David P, and Ben Kiernan, eds., *Revolution and Its Aftermath in Kampuchea: Eight Essays*. New Haven; Yale University Press, 1983.

Etcherson, Craig, *The Rise and Demise of Democratic Kampuchea*. Boulder; Westview, 1984.

Evans, Grant and Kelvin Rowley, eds., *Red Brotherhood at War: Vietnam, Laos and Cambodia Since 1975*. Rev. ed. London; Verso, 1990.

Heder, Stephen, *Kampuchean Occupation and Resistance*. Bangkok; Chulalongkorn University Press, 1980.

Jackson, Karl, ed., *Cambodia 1975-1978: Rendezvous with Death*. Princeton, N.J.; Princeton University Press, 1989.

Kiernan, Ben, *How Pol Pot Came to Power: A History of Communism in Kampuchea, 1930-1975*. London; Verso, 1985.

Kiernan, Ben, *The Pol Pot Regime; Race, Power and Genocide Under the Khmer Rouge, 1975-79* New Haven; Yale University Press, 1996.

Kiljunen, Kimmo, *Kampuchea: Dcade of the Genocide*. London, Zed Press, 1984.

Klintworth, Gary, *Vietnam's Intervention in International Law*. Canberra; Australian Government Publishing Service, 1989.

May, Someth, *Cambodian Witness: The Autobiography of Someth May*. London; Faber and Faber, 1988.

Ngor, Haing S., *Surviving the Killing Fields*. London; Chatto and Windus, 1988.

Osborne, Milton, *Sihanouk: Prince of Light, Prince of Darkness*. Honolulu; University of Hawaii Press, 1994.

Picq, Laurence, *Beyond the Horizon: Five Years With the Khmer Rouge*. Transl. by P. Norland. New York; St Martin's Press, 1989.

Vickery, Michael, *Cambodia 1975-1982*. London; South End Press, 1984.

Vickery, Michael, *Kampuchea: Politics, Economis and Society*. London; Pinter, 1986.

Yathay, Pin, *Stay Alive My Son*. New York; Free Press, 1987.

Contents

CHAPTER 1

The Evacuation of Phnom Penh

On the 17 April 1975, the government and armed forces of the Khmer Republic in Phnom Penh surrendered to the guerrillas of the Khmer Rouge revolutionary army. In the next day or two all provincial garrisons elsewhere in the country followed suit. The civil war that had devastated Kampuchea[1] for almost five years since the overthrow of Prince Norodom Sihanouk as Head of State in March 1970 was over. The country was at peace.

The final Khmer Rouge offensive against the capital had begun with the New Year. By 13 April Pochentong airport was closed, the American ambassador and his staff had fled, and it was only a matter of time before the beleaguered city was forced to capitulate. The atmosphere was heavy with foreboding and anticipation of what was about to take place. Rumour was rife; spirits rose in hope and were dashed in despair. When the end came on that warm, still Thursday morning, the overwhelming feeling was one of relief. No matter what the future might bring, the bloodshed and the fighting were over and Kampuchea could live again.

On the morning the Khmer Rouge entered Phnom Penh, Bunheang Ung and his family were up before six. Their house near the Independence Monument was on a corner opposite the headquarters of the Military Police. Bun could hear the crackle from the radio of a jeep parked beside the kerb. Soldiers were

The War is over.

monitoring the Khmer Rouge call for government forces to surrender, or face further bombardment from 107 mm rockets and artillery. Rockets had already caused terrible casualties and destruction, especially in the poorer areas where fires had destroyed thousands of wood and hessian dwellings. As the Khmer Rouge noose had drawn tighter, floods of refugees had choked the city; the population of Phnom Penh, estimated at as many as three million, was swollen to more than three times its prewar figure.[2]

Some time after 9 a.m. it became clear that the high command of the Republican armed forces was prepared to accept the demands for unconditional surrender. Some soldiers came to Bun's house to ask his mother for a piece of white material which they could attach to the aerial of their jeep. From their jokes and laughter, it was obvious that even the military police were happy that the war was over. There was almost a carnival atmosphere. The relief was tangible and when the first Khmer Rouge troops began entering the central city area, crowds applauded them. Trucks and cars loaded with young men blared horns and drove around aimlessly. Knots of people gathered on street corners. Men and women chatted and speculated and swapped the latest information.

While the first Khmer Rouge Bun saw seemed friendly and a little bewildered, those who followed were stern and unsmiling, suspicious of the welcome they received. Most were young, some very young. All wore black pyjamas, black-and-white check scarves hung around their necks (the kroma which serves the Kampuchean peasant as everything from a towel to a carrying sling). Soft black or olive-drab Chinese caps and Ho Chi Minh sandals cut from old motor tyres completed their uniform. They carried an assortment of weapons — Chinese AK-47 assault rifles, captured American M16s, anti-tank bazookas and pineapple grenades. They moved in single file, seemingly all but oblivious of the crowds of people clapping, calling to them, or curiously watching. Their demeanour was both alert and distrustful, like soldiers on patrol.

If Phnom Penh was enemy territory for the Khmer Rouge, these peasant guerrillas were just as alien to the inhabitants of the city. Remarkably little was known about the insurgents, or about their policies or plans for the nation. Despite government propaganda and occasional reports of torture and brutality, forced relocation of population and repression (often taken as propaganda), many people saw the Khmer Rouge in a positive light — as nationalists above all, fighting for a more just, less corrupt social order. Many hoped, despite indications to the contrary, that Prince Sihanouk still wielded some influence in the Royal Government of National Union of Kampuchea[3] set up as a government-in-exile in Beijing. But there was also widespread belief, fostered by the government of President Lon Nol, that the Khmer Rouge were creatures of the Vietnamese. Khmer Rouge victories were ascribed to Vietnamese support. When it became clear, as Khmer Rouge troops entered Phnom Penh, that no Vietnamese accompanied them, their nationalist image was reinforced. These were Khmer soldiers, brothers of the same race. With them agreement would be possible on the building of a new Kampuchea.

There were various reasons for the widespread ignorance in Phnom Penh about who the Khmer Rouge were and what they stood for.[4] Many of their leaders were known only under pseudonyms, *noms de guerre*. For long some of those who later proved to be among the top echelon of leadership, like Khieu Samphan, were believed to have been murdered years earlier by Sihanouk's secret police. Government propaganda was distrusted, and reports from the countryside discounted as rumour by the sophisticates of the capital. Also for every negative report there was a positive one — of Khmer Rouge justice, assistance for the peasants, scrupulous honesty and discipline, all in striking contrast to the behaviour of government forces. Both positive and negative reports could well have been true, for the Khmer Rouge did not comprise a monolithic organization. Much depended on the initiative of individual cadres. In many areas during the war, Khmer Rouge policies were less exacting than they were later to become — largely because the active support of the peasantry was essential both for recruitment into the guerrilla forces, and for supply of food and transportation of arms and equipment.

Like so many residents of the capital, the Ung family had received mixed reports of the Khmer Rouge. A distant uncle of Bun's had left the family's home village of Maesor Prachan in Peareang district, Prey Veng province, directly to the east of Phnom Penh, and brought his family to the capital in 1973. That was three years after the Khmer Rouge had first come to the village following General Lon Nol's rightwing *coup d'etat* against Sihanouk. The uncle was a small village merchant who considered that the socialist policies of the Khmer Rouge would make it difficult for him to earn a living in Maesor Prachan. But he had little criticism of the cadres he had encountered. They respected people, he told his family, and helped them when they

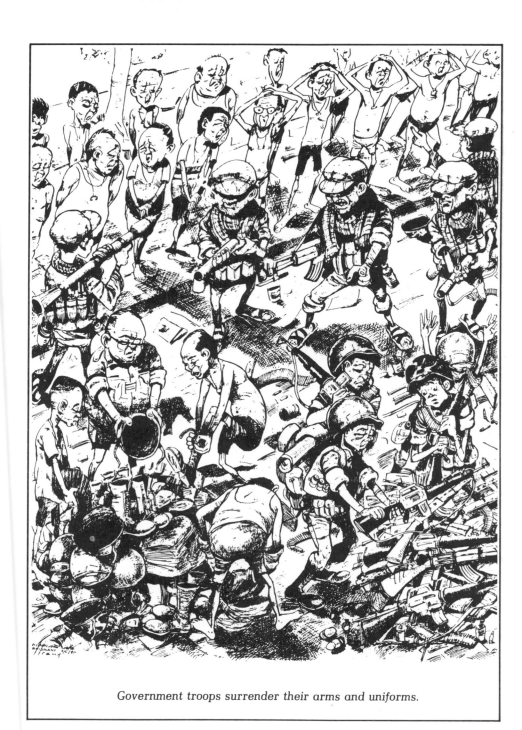

Government troops surrender their arms and uniforms.

were in need. He admitted that the Khmer Rouge were doing good things for the people, encouraging the setting up of cooperatives and generating a sense of pride and self reliance. But there was just no place in the new rural society they were creating for private business, so he had left.

Bun stayed in his house the morning of 17 April. He watched as a thin line of Khmer Rouge guerrillas arrived to accept the surrender of the jeep with the white flag and occupy the Military Police headquarters. The leader of the unit ordered all government troops to throw their weapons in a pile on the ground and to strip off their uniforms. His gestures were slow and reassuring. No attempt was made to collect the weapons. Government soldiers were told that fighting was at an end; all Khmer were brothers who should reunite in order to recover Khmer territory lost to the Vietnamese. The reference was to Kampuchea Krom, those parts of southern Vietnam which were once part of the Khmer empire during its great age of dominance over much of mainland southeast Asia and which were lost to Vietnam between the sixteenth and nineteenth centuries. For the next three and a half years this irredentist, anti-Vietnamese theme was to be relentlessly and suicidally pursued by the Khmer Rouge. In fact, despite Vietnamese statements welcoming the victory of the Kampuchean revolution, border provocations by Kampuchea against Vietnam began almost immediately.

Bun did not join the general rejoicing over the end of hostilities. He was more worried than happy, fearing his family with its business interests and professional connections would not find life easy in the new Kampuchea. Also he feared personal retribution. For some years, while studying at the Phnom Penh University of Fine Arts, he had worked part-time as a cartoonist for the independent newspaper Nokor Thom (the Great Country). The paper had critized both government policies and the Khmer Rouge, and Bun feared retaliation from the insurgents for poking fun at their pretensions. Finally he doubted whether an authoritarian communism was compatible with the national character of the Khmer people, a position he had adopted from the editor of Nokor Thom.

But if Bun had doubts about the Khmer Rouge, he had few about the regime of President Lon Nol. His dilemma was that of many Kampuchean students and intellectuals in Phnom Penh. Most had become increasingly disenchanted with the government's failure to come to grips with national problems, to counter the Khmer Rouge insurgency, to meet the popular demand for social justice, or to deal with corruption — in short, its failure to inspire and lead a national effort of rejuvenation and reconcilia-tion.[5] As a result of the government's failings, many of the capital's educated elite had adopted an attitude of resigned stoicism in the face of a likely Khmer Rouge victory. They knew that life would not be easy; but they felt that they too, no less than the Khmer Rouge, were Kampuchean nationalists. They would contribute as best they could to the rebuilding of the na-tion. Unlike the South Vietnamese elite, few middle-class profes-sional Kampucheans made any attempt to flee the country. For many who stayed, however, it was a tragic decision.

Even after the surrender of the Military Police head-quarters, Bun and his family did not join the expectant crowds in the street. They stayed in their house anxiously listening to the radio in the hope of learning what was happening. But after the official surrender announcement came soon after 10 a.m., Radio Phnom Penh played nothing but classical Khmer music. On the footpath outside, disarmed government soldiers stood in lines in their undershorts. About an hour later they climbed into trucks and were driven away, all but the few with families in Phnom Penh who had managed in the meantime to don civilian clothes and mingle with the crowds. No one knew where the soldiers who remained were taken. Only much later did Bun hear from friends that officers were driven to a mountainous area in Kompong Speu province, west of Phnom Penh, where they were massacred. Not until the overthrow of Pol Pot did the full extent of the early killing of politicians, government officials, army of-ficers and NCOs, intellectuals, teachers and students become clear. For more than three years Bun heard no whisper of these mass executions — only a rumour that high-ranking officials of the former regime were being held in a prison camp from which a few at a time were taken away and shot.

Before noon Khmer Rouge soldiers came to Bun's house and told the family to leave because, they said, the Americans were about to bomb Phnom Penh. "You must leave quickly", the Ung family was told. "Go fifteen or twenty kilometres away. Don't take much with you. You'll be back in two or three days. Don't bother to lock up, we shall look after everything until you return." Another reason given for the exodus was that the Khmer Rouge had to "clean up" the city. Some Lon Nol troops were refusing to surrender and had thrown grenades from win-dows. Bun could hear the sounds of intermittent firing as the Khmer Rouge flushed out small pockets of resistance with rockets and grenades. But few had the heart to fight on: only at one or two points did government troops put up a more determined resistance.

The Ung family had already packed a few essentials in anticipation of a hurried departure: food, cooking and eating utensils, clothing, torch and batteries, a radio, some books, personal papers, money, a little gold. They loaded everything into the family car a VW "beetle" driven by Bun's brother-in-law, Kylin Chy. As well as Kylin, there were his wife (Kim An), two of Bun's younger sisters, his seven-year-old brother and his mother, (Bun's father had died in 1971). Bun rode his 65 cc Honda. At the last minute Kylin ran back to fetch something he had forgotten. He was met by a young guerrilla who pointed a bazooka at his head and told him to go back. Kylin did not argue.

They drove painfully slowly through crowded streets and snarled traffic to Bun's grandparents' house. At such a time of crisis the family had to be together, to decide what should be done. The order for evacuation had come as a complete shock. People could not believe what was happening and they did not know where to go. Some sought advice from older relatives, others went to pagodas to consult the monks. The Khmer Rouge were clearing the city suburb by suburb. People moved ahead of them seeking friends and relatives — anything to avoid leaving the city which they knew and where they felt secure. Some tried to hide in their own homes so that the Khmer Rouge would not know they were there, but most were discovered and forced to leave. Some who argued were shot. One or two Chinese merchants in the commercial centre of the city barricaded their shops with heavy steel shutters, but the Khmer Rouge used bazookas to blast their way in. Owners were chased into the street while their premises were systematically smashed and merchandise thrown into the street.

The Ung family stayed the night of the seventeenth at the house of Bun's grandfather, Polay Ung. That evening they talked endlessly over what was happening and why, of what the Khmer Rouge intended, and whether the Americans would bomb the city. In the morning Khmer Rouge troops ordered them to leave immediately. Bun's grandfather declared that this was his home: he would not leave, even if he had to die there. Besides he had to find his wife who had been visiting relatives. As Polay Ung expostulated with the young guerrillas, a boy whom Bun took to be no more than thirteen or fourteen years old raised his pistol, fired into the air, and repeated the order to leave. The old man, visibily shaken, tottered into the street. Hurriedly the family decided on the best road to take and it was agreed they should

Khmer Rouge troops exercise their authority.

The exodus from Phnom Penh.

head in the direction of their home village, Maesor Prachan. They would take the Monivong Bridge across the Bassac River, on National Route One linking Phnom Penh to Saigon. Hopefully they would be able to camp for a couple of days outside the city, and then return, as the Khmer Rouge had promised.

The family left in three cars — the VW, Polay Ung's tiny Honda, and a Peugeot 404 belonging to Bun's widowed aunt who lived with his grandparents. Everything they might need was packed into the cars, including any valuables which they feared would be looted. It took until six that evening to reach the bridge, and more than six hours to cross it, inching forward in the crush of people, cars, bicycles, carts, cyclopousses, anything on which could be loaded a few belongings, a sack of rice. Those who had cars usually pushed them a few metres at a time, to conserve petrol.

In that mass evacuation of a city swollen with refugees, and with the sick and wounded of a war where no quarter was given, callousness, cruelty, suffering and despair compounded the sense of shock and disorientation which the command to leave had produced. The order was carried out with blind single-mindedness, by peasant soldiers hardened by war and inured to a harsh and merciless discipline in the name of their revolution. They had been trained to obey without question, to the death. They had watched their comrades die, slogging through the morass of paddy mud, in the face of murderous counter fire, under the terrifyingly destructive rain of American aerial bombardment. The guerrillas had come to believe that those they fought were not real Khmer, but people who had sold their souls to a foreign power, to American imperialism, to those who saw the war in Kampuchea as a mere sideshow to the conflict in Vietnam. Their orders were to evacuate Phonm Penh, and every provincial city and town, completely, without exception; and they carried out those orders to the letter. No pleading, no pain could touch them. Hospitals were emptied. The sick were carried on stretchers, in the arms of relatives. Cripples, the incapacitated, those who had lost limbs from land mines or rocket fire, all joined the slowly moving throngs pouring along the main arteries north, east, south and west out of the city. Virtually the whole population was on the move. Families separated at the time of surrender remained separated. Parents in one part of the city were prevented from seeking their children elsewhere. Bun's grandmother was somewhere with his uncle's family, but everyone was forced to take the nearest evacuation route. Those whose home villages were in another direction could only hope to circle around the capital once they reached the countryside, a detour that would take days of difficult walking along village tracks, carrying loads of belongings, sleeping in the open, eating whatever they could find.

In that respect the Ung family was fortunate. Their nearest route of exit from the city was to the south, then west across the Bassac. They had only to cross the Mekong to be on their way to the family's ancestral village of Maesor Prachan. But progress was glacially slow: at first as little as 500 metres in a day as those further from the city slowed down, waiting for the word to return, and others banked up behind them.

The second night Bun's family camped, exhausted, at 3 a.m., on the verge of the highway some distance from the Monivong bridge. For the next few days they moved on slowly, staying near the river where they could obtain water and fish, and buy vegetables from local peasants at grossly inflated prices.

The first two or three days of the exodus left an indelible impression on those who took part.[7] In the heat the bodies of those killed in the last days of fighting swelled up and began to rot. Everywhere hung the sweet sickening stench of death; but no-one attempted to bury the dead. Khmer Rouge guerrillas urged people to keep moving. Occasionally a young cadre would fire into the air. But few needed such encouragement: people were sufficiently terrified by the power of life and death that every Khmer Rouge soldier apparently exercised. Some of the actions of these young soldiers seemed quite arbitrary. Youths with long hair could be arrested for no apparent reason except their appearance. Long hair symbolized all the the Khmer Rouge hated most, the corruption of American imperialist culture and the aimless and unproductive leisure of an exploitative class of urban parasites. On the Monivong bridge Bun saw one such youth on a motor bike stopped and shot in cold blood. The body was casually dumped over the side of the bridge. Other youths were led away with a rope around the neck, together with anyone suspected of being an officer in the Republican army, or a high-ranking civil official. Although Bun's hair was not very long, his aunt insisted on immediately cutting it shorter.

All along the road thousands upon thousands of people camped as best they could, surrounded by their belongings, cooking meagre supplies of food. The Ung family had taken only three bags of rice and the price of food rose daily, quadrupling within two days and thereafter rising rapidly until it was more than ten times the pre-evacuation price. Costs for meat and vegetables rose even more rapidly. Hygiene was appalling, medicine almost

On the road from the capital.

Checkpoint at Koki.

unobtainable — though Bun did once see some Khmer Rouge distributing a few simple drugs to those evidently sick. The seriously ill died where they lay. Most were old people or very young and sick children abandoned by families already laden down with all they could carry. Yet in all this chaos and confusion, the Ung family miraculously met up with two uncles and their families, including Bun's grandmother. It was a happy reunion. His uncles had had the same idea as Bun's family — head towards the one village in Kampuchea which they knew and where they might feel secure.

At Koki, about seventeen kilometres from the city, the Khmer Rouge had set up a checkpoint where everyone was searched and questioned. Here Bun was interrogated closely. A young guerrilla looked him over carefully and demanded if he were a soldier. Bun insisted he was only a student, and after showing his student card he was allowed to pass. A loudspeaker was calling on all military officers to report to the new authorities in order to help build a new army. A line of Republican officers was being led away by black-clad cadres. Bun pleaded with his cousin, a lieutenant, not to give himself up. But his cousin insisted it was his duty: he was needed for the service of his country. They never saw him again.[8]

Even at Koki, however, not everyone was subjected to a body search. The Ung family passed the checkpoint after dark, and Bun managed to hide his watch and a small radio. Cars and baggage were searched, apparently for arms. Many belongings were confiscated: anything suspected of being army issue, such as blankets, or boots; any electrical appliances, radios, tape recorders or record players; watches, cameras, books; anything which might recall the "old society" which the Khmer Rouge were determined to replace. Photographs were torn up, as were any documents or diplomas. Bun's sister lost her chemistry diploma. Everything was thrown into heaps and trampled into the mud. Even medicines were confiscated: the Ung family lost those aspirin and antibiotics they had not hidden. No-one questioned the decision of the Khmer Rouge, even when it was clear that most of the young soldiers could not read the papers they destroyed.

Many people were arrested at this check point, especially those suspected of formerly being in the military. Denials were often ignored: a Khmer Rouge slogan asserted that it was better to make a thousand mistakes than let one person who should be detained go undetected. Anyone with a tattoo was automatically seized as likely to have been in the army. Bun watched as a fat man was hauled from his car and arrested on a charge of being either a general, or an exploiter of the people. Judgment appeared to be on his size alone.

Some of the things confiscated were not immediately destroyed as imperialist junk. They were set aside for use by Angkar Loeu — literally "The Higher Organization" — the term universally used by Khmer Rouge cadres (kamaphibal) or soldiers (yotheas) to refer collectively to all echelons of the revolutionary command structure. Cadres and soldiers themselves constituted the lowest level of Angkar. When any cadre or soldier wanted to appropriate something from an evacuee, he always "proposed" that it should be made available for use by Angkar. When a young guerrilla told Bun that Angkar proposed that he surrender his motorcycle, there was nothing for it but to comply. Such a proposal was an order, as anyone unwilling to part with a possession soon discovered. Reference to Angkar enabled any cadre to take from any evacuee whatever took his fancy. Soon most cadres possessed such items as watches, ball-point pens, radios, bicycles and cassette recorders, though many were later forced to surrender them for communal use.

After passing through the Koki checkpoint, the Ung family drove on a few kilometres and set up camp, waiting to be told to return to Phnom Penh. They were still there ten days after leaving the city when they heard a radio broadcast calling upon everyone to go to their home villages. Food stocks in the capital were exhausted. The new regime had no means to bring in supplies but there was rice in the villages, and the opportunity for everyone to gather and grow more food. The Ung family were luckier than many whose only home was Phonm Penh and who were sometimes forced to wander from village to village until one would accept them. They were within thirty kilometres of Maesor Prachan. But the village lay north, across the Mekong. There was nothing for it but to abandon the cars, take whatever they could carry, pay to be ferried across the river, and begin walking.

It took the thirty-five men, women and children in the extended Ung family two more weeks to reach their village. The sacks of belongings and food that each member carried made progress very slow. Rest stops were frequent, especially as one of Bun's aunts was eight months pregnant. At night they slept on the ground, or in abandoned houses or pagodas. Often it rained. By the time they reached Maesor Prachan, their food supplies were finished, and they wanted only to rest. But Angkar decided otherwise.

The evacuation of Phnom Penh was unprecedented.[9] Never before had a city of three million people been emptied of its inhabitants in this way. Why did the Khmer Rouge order this exodus?

Ieng Sary, Vice Premier in charge of Foreign Affairs in the new government of Democratic Kampuchea, told reporters at the Conference of Non-Aligned States, held at Lima, in 1975 that the reasons for the evacuation were economic and humanitarian. He repeated the claim that because there was no food in Phnom Penh and the new government had no means of transportation, the population had to be dispersed to prevent massive starvation. No mention was made of reports that the U.S. would bomb the city. But if the evacuation was ordered on humanitarian grounds, why force the elderly, sick and wounded to leave? There is no doubt some food could have been brought to Phnom Penh by boat down the Mekong. The only excuse provided by those who have defended the decision has been to claim that the young Khmer Rouge guerrillas, trained to absolute obedience under wartime conditions, lacked the necessary judgment to make exceptions for special cases. They were told to evacuate the city, and that is what they did. But this too is unconvincing. The rank-and-file of Khmer Rouge may have been young and inexperienced, but their leaders had successfully conducted a large-scale war. It would not have been too difficult to send responsible cadres at least to the major hospitals to decide who could stay.

A more likely reason for the evacuation concerns security. This was hinted at by the Khmer Rouge when they told people it was necessary to "clean up" the city before allowing anyone to return. Cadres did not elaborate on what they meant by "clean up", but the CIA undoubtedly had its agents and informers in Phnom Penh. So too did the Vietnamese and, incidentally, the Chinese, each predominantly among their respective ethnic communities in the capital. Opponents of the new regime could more easily go underground in a city they knew; the former civil service and the business elite could more easily have maintained their networks of family relationships and contacts in Phnom Penh. These informal networks were broken up and people found themselves in villages they did not know, among people they could not trust. They were fearful, disoriented, dependent on others. Under these circumstances, no central focus of opposition to the new regime could develop.

But perhaps the prime motivation for the evacuation was the regime's ideological commitment to the creation of a one-class state. Evacuation of the capital was designed to remould the Kampuchean urban population. Manual work would transform them into labourers on agricultural communes and thus overcome at a single stroke every distinction of class and status. The importance of this ideological consideration is borne out by the evacuation of even small provincial towns, and by the ruthlessness with which the entire operation was carried out. The aim was to produce a new Kampuchea consisting of a single class of agricultural producers, unified in their devotion to Angkar and the Kampuchean state. The surplus produced by this agricultural labour force would permit the regime to attain the goal of an entirely independent and self-sufficient Kampuchean economy free from all foreign manipulation.

Security and commitment to an ideology of radical egalitarianism seem on balance to have been the principal reasons for the evacuation. Both were combined in the explanation given to the engineer Pin Yathay by a ranking district Khmer Rouge cadre in Takeo province some time later. The official told Pin:

> We know that it is dangerous to leave the towns intact and inhabited. They are the centres for opposition and small groups opposed to the regime. In a town it is difficult to track down these counter-revolutionary cells. If city life is not modified, an enemy organization can reconstitute itself and align itself against us. It is truly impossible to control a town. We have evacuated the towns in order to overcome all resistance, to destroy the cradle of reactionary and mercantile capitalism. To expel the town dwellers is to eliminate the germ of anti-Khmer Rouge resistance.[10]

However, there may have been yet another reason for the exodus, one which had to do with the belief in a kind of semi-mystical renewal of the Khmer race that formed an unacknowledged part of Khmer Rouge thinking. Cities were evil and corrupt, parasitically drawing their sustenance from the countryside like a tumour in the body of the nation. They were also conduits for the foreign influence which had sapped the pristine strength of the Khmer people. Purification of those contaminated by city life could only come through physical contact with the land itself. Only through labouring in the Khmer soil, so it was believed, could the racial and cultural purity of the Khmer people be renewed and sustained.

Whatever the reason, the evacuation of Phnom Penh and provincial towns ranks as one of the greatest single movements of population in modern times. The suffering it caused was immense: no-one will ever know how many people died as a direct result of this decision. It is certain, however, that hundreds literally walked to their deaths — the sick, the wounded, the very old, and the very young. All who took part in that evacuation saw bodies left along the roadside, buried in shallow graves, or tossed into a river.[11] The evacuation involved the total urban population of Kampuchea, which at one time numbered well in excess of three million. This included, in addition to the population of the capital, the populations of major provincial towns such as Battambang and Siem Reap each also swollen with refugees, and the populations of those few smaller towns and villages which remained under government control. Of this total number, some 200,000 were ethnic Vietnamese who were immediately forcibly repatriated to Vietnam. An even larger number were ethnic Chinese, who, however, were treated as Kampucheans and resettled in villages.

Executions during the evacuation period of former Republican army officers, high-ranking civil servants, and any who disobeyed or even questioned Khmer Rouge orders, are also almost impossible to estimate. Not all the 20,000 or more army officers were killed, though most of those who were not were subsequently executed. Of the 30,000 civil servants, few seem to have been killed at first, though many died later. Lower ranking functionaries more often escaped with their lives. Students and teachers were not targets for execution at first, though many of these too were later killed. It is unlikely that more than a few people were shot for arguing or disobeying orders since it took only one or two examples for everyone else to obey.

On the basis of these figures, it seems possible that as many as 35,000 Kampucheans could have died during the first month of the Khmer Rouge regime.

This is an appallingly high figure; but it amounts to no more than a fraction of some estimates (including one by the CIA) which have put the number of dead as high as 400,000 in those first few weeks, a figure which has been shown to be wildly exaggerated.[12] Far more were to die later, of starvation and disease, through pogroms and purges, as a result of mass relocation of population and the war with Vietnam, or while trying to flee the country. The deaths of all stand as an everlasting indictment of the Khmer Rouge regime.

CHAPTER 2

Who Is Angkar?

What was the nature of a regime that could, apparently without compunction, inflict such suffering on so many of its own people during less than four years in power? In April 1975 the mass of the Kampuchean people had only a hazy idea of either the immediate policies or the longer-term programme of Angkar Loeu.[1] The organization itself, and the identity of most of its leaders, remained a mystery. All that even educated Kampucheans, and the outside world, knew of the leadership of the Khmer revolution was the membership of the Royal Government of National Union of Kampuchea, under the nominal leadership of Prince Sihanouk. Both the government-in-exile and the National United Front leading the struggle in Kampuchea included anti-communists loyal to Sihanouk who had refused to support the military coup of General Lon Nol against the Prince in 1970, together with former leftist opponents of Sihanouk who had previously joined the underground resistance against his government. These disparate groups were united only in their determined opposition to the Lon Nol regime, and their relationship within the National United Front was far from clear. In reality, by the time the Khmer Rouge took Phnom Penh, Sihanouk was little more than a remote figurehead living in Beijing: real power lay in the hands of the Communist Party of Kampuchea (CPK).

Since 1979, much more information has come to light both on the origins of the Kampuchean communist movement, and on tensions within the CPK and its front organizations. We now know something about the background to the communist victory in Kampuchea.

The first communist activity dates from the early 1930s when a few ethnic Khmer joined Ho Chi Minh's Indochina Communist Party (ICP). Left-wing nationalism did not gain momentum, however, until the arrival of Japanese forces in Kampuchea in 1940, and the occupation, with Japanese consent, of the two western Kampuchean provinces of Battambang and Siem Reap by Thai troops. Resistance to the Japanese, the Thai, and to French colonialism was organized by Khmer nationalists, including members of the ICP, who called themselves the Khmer Issarak (the Free or Independent Khmers). In 1945 a Japanese-backed Khmer government proclaimed Kampuchean independence from France, but was unable to prevent the return of French forces to Phnom Penh.

By the end of the war the Khmer Issarak controlled as much as 40 per cent of the country. During the next nine years many Issarak cadres worked closely with the Vietminh in their joint struggle for independence from France. Already at this time, however, the leadership of the Kampuchean revolutionary movement was divided over how close relations should be with the Vietnamese. In April 1950 a Unified Issarak Front was formed to coordinate all resistance activities against the French. ICP members who favoured closer cooperation with the Vietminh held a number of important positions in the Front, and Vietnamese communist assistance was rapidly channelled into building up the Kampuchean liberation movement. With the formal abolition of the ICP in 1951, a Khmer People's Revolutionary Party was formed, forerunner to the CPK. It was not, strictly speaking, a Marxist-Leninist party, but drew its support from a broad cross-section of the nationalist left. By 1954 it had command, through the United Issarak Front, of some 3,500 troops (not including local guerrilla forces) in control, once again, of some two-fifths of the national territory.

In 1953 young Prince Sihanouk, whom the French had installed as traditional ruler of Kampuchea, took the wind out of the sails of the revolutionary left by proclaiming himself leader of the Kampuchean independence movement and negotiating independence from France. At one stroke the United Issarak Front was deprived of its stated reason for fighting. As leader of an already independent state, Sihanouk could argue at Geneva in 1954 that his government represented a united and independent country. There was no need, therefore, for provision to be made to regroup leftist guerrillas in separate areas already under their administration, as happened in Laos and in the division of Vietnam. Though this deprived the Kampuchean revolutionary left of a power base, socialist-bloc countries, including both the Soviet Union and the People's Republic of China, accepted it as part of the overall settlement known as the Geneva Agreements on Indochina. This sacrifice of their interests made a deep impression on future leaders of the radical left in Kampuchea, for it was taken to show that even their "friends" were prepared to betray them, if it was in their interest to do so.[2]

The Geneva Agreements left Kampuchean leftists who had actively sided with the Vietminh with three choices: to withdraw with their Vietnamese allies to North Vietnam; to remain underground in Kampuchea; or (most risky of all) to form a radical-socialist opposition party to contest elections in 1955 against Sihanouk's own party, the Sangkum Reastre Niyum (People's Socialist Community). Estimates differ on the number who went north, but probably between one and two thousand left in 1954, a few of whom returned to rejoin those working in the Khmer underground.[3] A handful of former Issarak leaders organized the Pracheachon (Sovereign People's Party), which, despite considerable support in some areas, failed to win a single seat in the 1955 elections. Other members of the Issarak Front gave up active politics altogether.

The late 1950s were a time of repression for the radical left in Kampuchea. International acceptance of Kampuchean neutrality and the new Soviet policy of peaceful coexistence left Sihanouk free to seek out and exterminate suspected communists. Communication between the underground in Kampuchea and cadres in North Vietnam was difficult, if not impossible. Aided by defections and betrayal, Sihanouk's secret police had by 1959 destroyed most of the rural underground. As a result of this loss of experienced rural cadres (through assassination, imprisonment or flight to North Vietnam), by the time the second congress of the Khmer People's Revolutionary Party was held in 1960, the Phnom Penh committee — composed largely of young urban intellectuals — had come to wield disproportionate influence.

In the early 1950s a number of Cambodian students studying in France had become Marxists. These included Saloth Sar (alias Pol Pot), Ieng Sary and Khieu Samphan, whose doctoral thesis in economics entitled "Cambodia's Economy and Industrial Development" appeared in 1959. The thesis foreshadowed, as a means of freeing Kampuchea from its third World economic

Pol Pot.

dependency, many of the economic policies later to be enforced by the Khmer Rouge. Saloth Sar returned to Kampuchea in time to take part briefly in the anti-French resistance in August 1953. Other students including Ieng Sary, returned after independence directly to Phnom Penh. In the new Central Committee formed at the 1960 congress, Pol Pot (then still known as Saloth Sar) was promoted to become the third member of the three-man politburo, together with Secretary-General Tou Samouth and his deputy Nuon Chea. Of the five additional full members of the Central Committee, two were Phnom Penh students, two were in North Vietnam, and only one, So Phim, was a veteran revolutionary still active in the rural underground. The name of the Party was changed to the Worker's Party of Kampuchea to mark the formation of a more genuinely Marxist-Leninist party, and changed again in 1966 to the Communist Party of Kampuchea.

When Party Secretary Tou Samouth disappeared in 1962 (presumably killed by Sihanouk's police), Pol Pot became acting secretary, a position which was confirmed at the hastily-called 1963 Congress. At the same time, former students Ieng Sary and Vorn Veth were promoted to the enlarged Politburo, along with So Phim.[4] This congress therefore marked the ascendancy in the party hierarchy (a) of French-educated Phnom Penh-based intellectuals over veteran rural revolutionaries; and (b) of Party members remaining in Kampuchea over those who had regrouped in North Vietnam. Both these developments were important for the subsequent direction and development of the Khmer revolution.

Within a few months of the 1963 congress, Pol Pot, Ieng Sary, Son Sen, and other urban communists were forced to flee Phnom Penh for the relative safety of the northeastern ethnic minority areas close to the southern terminus of the Ho Chi Minh trail.[5] Other more moderate leftists, including Khieu Samphan, remained in Phnom Penh for another three years. They were enabled to do this because of Sihanouk's policy of differentiating between the moderate and radical left: while the radicals were targets for police repression, the moderates were incorporated into the left-wing of the Prince's Sangkum Party. Only after unrepresentative elections in 1966 returned a parliament dominated by the conservative right were moderate leftists squeezed out of the Sangkum. When in March and April 1967 a peasant rebellion broke out in the Samlaut region of Battambang province in response to the forced collection of rice by the National Army, this was seized upon by the government as evidence of left-wing agitation. A new wave of repression followed, forcing many moderate leftist teachers and students to join the maquis for fear of their lives.

Early in 1968 communist organizers exploited continuing peasant discontent in Battambang to incite a new uprising. This was again put down with much brutality by government forces under General Lon Nol.[6] From this time dates the CPK decision to resort to armed struggle, a decision severely critized at the time by the Vietnamese. For the next two years, however, until the military coup against Sihanouk, the CPK was forced to place most emphasis on political propaganda and mobilization. During this period, membership of the People's Movement of United Resistance, a broad political front for the CPK, increased to somewhere around 10,000, less than half of whom were armed. They were scathingly referred to by Sihanouk as the Khmer Rouge, the "Red Khmer".

In 1965 Sihanouk, concerned over the rising tide of war in South Vietnam and the possibility of Kampuchea becoming embroiled, decided to sever diplomatic ties with the United States and improve relations with the Democratic Republic of [North] Vietnam (DRV) and the National Front for the Liberation of South Vietnam. He permitted Vietnamese Communist forces to establish bases on the Kampuchean side of the border, where they received plentiful supplies of arms and equipment from the north, along the Ho Chi Minh trail. More supplies came in by ship via the port of Sihanoukville, with Kampuchean government blessing. Such positive neutrality suited Hanoi. In return the Vietnamese limited their assistance to the Kampuchean insurgents by refusing to supply the CPK with arms.

The later 1960s were a crucial period in the development of relations between the CPK and the communist leaders of North Vietnam. In 1965 and 1966 Pol Pot secretly visited both Beijing and Hanoi, where he undoubtedly met with expatriate members of the CPK Central Committee. In Beijing Pol Pot met Mao Zedong and other Chinese leaders. He reportedly stayed in China for about four months, just prior to the Cultural Revolution, and received considerable encouragement. We can only speculate with what enthusiasm and conviction Pol Pot returned to Kampuchea, how he reacted to Vietnamese determination to place their own revolution before that of Kampuchea, and what he thought of Vietnamese policies towards both the Sihanouk regime and the communist movement in Kampuchea. Something of the Kampuchean response is revealed in the Black Paper which the Khmer Rouge issued in 1978, detailing "acts of aggression, and annexation of Vietnam against Kampuchea". There it is obvious how deeply the Vietnamese policy of restraint in Kampuchea had rankled Khmer Rouge leaders. As early as 1966, the Black Paper claims, "the Communist Party of Kampuchea consolidated and strengthened its position of independence, sovereignty and self-reliance, and clearly discerned the true nature of the Vietnamese".[7]

At the same time as dissatisfaction with the Vietnamese grew, CPK leaders came under the increasingly radical influence of the Chinese Cultural Revolution. This influence was especially strong among those intellectuals, such as Hu Nim and Phouk Chhay, who joined the maquis in 1966 and 1967, and who until then had been active members of the Khmer-Chinese Friendship Association in Phnom Penh. These men were attracted by the ideology of "mass democracy", self-reliance, and radical socio-economic change espoused by the Red Guards.

The experience of the leadership of the CPK during these years of frustration and condescending treatment by the Vietnamese led to growing suspicion over long-term Vietnamese intentions towards Kampuchea. Were the Vietnamese still intent on establishing a "Federation of Indochina" to include a united Vietnam, Laos and Kampuchea controlled from Hanoi?[8] Even the suggestion that this might be so was enough to revive ancient Khmer fears of political annexation and cultural assimilation at the hands of the more numerous and assertive Vietnamese. Had not the Mekong delta provinces of southern Vietnam once been part of the Kampuchean empire, and Saigon the Khmer provincial capital of Prey Nokor? And had not Vietnamese emperors exercised political sway in Kampuchea before the arrival of the French? The leadership of the CPK was determined above all to maintain national independence. In their estimation, this historic national goal was a goal of the revolution itself: only through revolution could the nation be sufficiently strengthened to withstand what they came to see as continuing Vietnamese expansionism. It would seem that "the true nature of the Vietnamese" which CPK leaders discerned in 1966 was that "fraternal" Vietnamese communists were as eager to exercise political influence in Kampuchea as their feudal ancestors had been.

Then in March 1970 came the overthrow of Sihanouk by General Lon Nol while the Prince was on holiday in France. But the establishment of a pro-American right-wing government dedicated to expelling every Vietnamese communist from Kampuchean territory actually played into the hands of the CPK.[9] Incensed at Lon Nol's treachery, Sihanouk flew to Beijing where he entered into negotiations with Khmer Rouge representatives to set up a common resistance front with his former adversaries. As a result of these negotiations, the National United Front was formed to include supporters of Sihanouk. The CPK could now claim to be fighting on behalf of Kampuchea's rightful head of state.

Within a week the first peasant demonstrations in support of Sihanouk occurred. These grew quickly and were met by repression from Lon Nol's army — hundreds of unarmed peasants were killed. Sihanouk still enjoyed an almost divine status in the eyes of many Kampuchean peasants, a status which Lon Nol, as the new President of the Khmer Republic, could not usurp. However, these peasant demonstrations were somewhat surprising, as the principal centres of unrest were precisely those where the Khmer Rouge were strongest. In other words, the demonstrations should probably be seen not so much as manifestations of spontaneous support for Sihanouk, but rather as the first use by the Khmer Rouge of Sihanouk's name for their own ends.[10]

The military coup destroyed any rationale Hanoi had for restraining the Khmer Rouge from launching a full-scale armed insurgency against the Kampuchean government. Until then, forces of the Vietnam People's Army (VPA) based in Kampuchea in camps a few kilometres from the Vietnamese border had co-existed, though uneasily, with the small, poorly-led, Khmer National Army. When it became obvious that the Lon Nol government intended to permit American and South Vietnamese troops to attack Vietnamese communist forces in Kampuchea (something Sihanouk had never permitted them to do), the Vietnamese moved to secure their lines of retreat. Some VPA units moved back up the Ho Chi Minh trail into Laos; others withdrew further into Kampuchea, sweeping away National Army garrisons and making over large areas to the Khmer insurgents. When the American-South Vietnamese invasion came in May, its only lasting effect was greatly to increase the power and presence of the Khmer Rouge in areas previously under government control. When the Americans withdrew, VPA and Khmer Rouge forces returned to the border region where they eliminated all remaining Khmer National Army presence, first from the countryside, then from the smaller towns. The rich rice growing provinces of eastern Kampuchea progressively fell under the control of the Khmer Rouge.

After the coup against Sihanouk, most of the so-called "Khmer Vietminh" returned to Kampuchea from North Vietnam. These were the communists who had fled to North Vietnam in the late 1950s where they had undergone years of political training and indoctrination. A few had joined the Khmer Rouge in the northeast during the following decade, usually in a liaison capacity with the Vietnamese. As such they had argued for the Vietnamese line of support for Sihanouk's policy of Kampuchean neutrality in return for the Prince's acceptance of Vietnamese communist bases on Kampuchean soil. But by their failure to support an active armed insurgency in Kampuchea, these cadres had earned the suspicion of the self-styled "domestic" in-country leadership of the CPK. By the time the remainder returned the Khmer Vietminh were already seen as agents for Vietnamese designs on Kampuchea and were consequently systematically prevented from gaining influential positions in the CPK. Thus by refusing to support the Khmer revolution in the 1960s, and by keeping the Khmer Vietminh in North Vietnam, the Vietnamese had in effect allowed the CPK to fall under the control of a radical nationalist leadership far from sympathetic to Vietnamese interests.

The Vietnamese clearly hoped to influence the Khmer revolution through the Khmer Vietminh they had so carefully trained. In another attempt to limit the power of the domestic leadership of the CPK, Hanoi also helped train and equip a force of Eastern Zone recruits under the command of a former monk called Chan Chakrey. These wore jungle-green fatigue uniforms and were known as Khmer Rumdoah (Liberation Khmer), or Khmer Blanc (White Khmer) to distinguish them from the black-clad guerrillas of the Khmer Khrahom (Red Khmer, or Khmer Rouge). During the war against Lon Nol, relations between the two groups were often strained since the Khmer Rumdoah were not under the control of the CPK Central Committee and thus posed a threat to the monolithic control of the Party.

For the five years from 1970 to 1975 the domestic leadership of the CPK pursued three simultaneous goals: elimination of their political rivals (both the Khmer Vietminh within the Party, and the Khmer Rumdoah and other supporters of Sihanouk); defeat of the Lon Nol government and its armed forces; and the beginnings of socialist transformation of Kampuchean society. The first was all but accomplished by early 1973; the second took two years longer; and the third, though well under way in some areas by 1975, was still being actively pursued when the Pol Pot regime was overthrown in January 1979.

The elimination of political rivals was aimed above all at the elimination of Vietnamese influence in the Kampuchean revolution. Until about the middle of 1971, the Khmer Rouge were still dependent on Vietnamese assistance. As villages were liberated from government control, new local administrations were set up, often with Vietnamese assistance. Vietnamese troops were careful to provide no cause for friction; they respected Khmer customs, and were particularly strict in their behaviour towards women and Buddhist monks. Vietnamese cadres helped organize village militias to resist the Lon Nol government, particularly in the east and southeast along the Vietnamese border. Material assistance not only for the Khmer Rumdoah, but also for the Khmer Rouge, flowed in from Vietnam.

By late 1971, the leaders of the Kampuchean revolution felt strong enough to reduce their dependency on the Vietnamese. A decision was taken at a secret meeting of the Central Committee to expel all Vietnamese troops from Kampuchea, and to eliminate the Khmer Vietminh. Apparently this decision was supported even by those domestic CPK leaders who had benefited most from Vietnamese assistance in the past. The Khmer communists were determined to retain sole control of their revolution and the Vietnamese trained veteran revolutionaries were considered a divisive influence within the party. Vietnam itself was even then seen as the "acute enemy" of Kampuchea.

Khmer Vietminh veterans were progressively reassigned from administrative to military duties, where they were often given suicidal missions. Others were secretly executed by the State Security apparatus (Santebal). By the end of 1971 as many as half of those who had returned from North Vietnam the previous year were dead. Most of the rest were purged the previous year were dead. Many of the rest were purged the following year. A few, realizing their danger, managed to flee to the northwest, where they survived until the purges of 1976 and 1977.

By the end of 1972 the Vietnamese had to accept the fact that they had lost any influence they might once have had within the CPK. "Spontaneous" demonstrations against the continued presence of Vietnamese forces in Kampuchea had been followed in 1972 by fighting between VPA and Khmer Rouge troops. In order to avoid increasingly frequent clashes with the Khmer Rouge, Vietnamese communist forces began to withdraw from the eastern areas of Kampuchea. This left the Kampuchean resistance forces to settle their scores. By May 1973, the Khmer Rouge had begun a concerted purge of pro-Sihanouk elements from all positions of authority in the villages of eastern and southwestern Kampuchea. Towards the end of 1973 fighting broke out between Khmer Rouge and Khmer Rumdoah military units over control of the rice crop in Kampot province. As the Khmer Rouge gradually gained the upper hand, thousands of pro-Sihanouk peasants fled across the border into South Vietnam.

The events of 1973 were crucial for the subsequent phase of the power struggle within the CPK, which eventually saw the triumph of the radical nationalist faction identified with Pol Pot. In January that year, North Vietnam and the United States signed a ceasefire agreement. In Laos the Pathet Lao followed the Vietnamese example, but in Kampuchea the Khmer Rouge refused all offers of negotiation. This left the Kampuchean insurgents to fight on alone and the awesome and terrifying power of U.S. aerial warfare was thus reserved entirely for Kampuchea. Between February and August 1973, when the bombing finally stopped, over 250,000 tons of bombs had been dropped, more than one and a half times the tonnage dropped on Japan throughout the entire Second World War.[11]

Under this rain of bombs, the Khmer Rouge tightened their grip over the Kampuchean peasantry. The Party saw the struggle in apocalyptic terms: everything had to be sacrificed to the revolution. All youths of sixteen or over were forcibly recruited into the Khmer Rouge armed forces, where they were subjected to intensive propaganda. In some areas under Khmer Rouge control anyone evading conscription could be shot. Complete obedience to the instructions of the Party was demanded. Any refusal to comply was dealt with by arrest, imprisonment, and either slow death through disease and maltreatment, or execution. The atmosphere of terror generated by these methods was a potent force in the Khmer Rouge programme of total mobilization for total war. Some who could, fled — either to South Vietnam or to the diminishing government-controlled areas. Most stayed because they had no alternative. Control over personal movement was extremely strict, with permission necessary merely to visit a neighbouring village, one reason perhaps why Khmer Rouge policies were so little known or understood outside the regions under their control during the war years.

In July 1973 the Khmer Rouge mounted a poorly coordinated attack on Phnom Penh in a bid to win the war. Forces advancing from the southwest bore the brunt of the U.S. bombing and suffered appalling casualties. This attack on Phnom Penh has been described as "a madness born of desperate isolation, which bred a dreadful hatred of their enemy and a contempt for the attitudes of the outside world".[12] It convinced the Party leadership that nothing short of total commitment would bring victory, and so added to the brutality and xenophobia of the regime.

One immediate effect was to intensify the Party's determination to destroy any remaining support for Sihanouk inside Kampuchea. This led to more armed clashes between Khmer Rouge troops and the few remaining Khmer Rumdoah units, which resulted in the virtual elimination of the latter by early 1974. Another effect was to increase hatred of the Vietnamese and to weaken the position of anyone in the CPK who was still prepared to take Vietnamese communism as a model for communism in Kampuchea. As well, the failure of the attack on Phnom Penh lead to the replacement of the Southwest Zone Chairman by his military commander, Ta Mok, a supporter of Pol Pot, who proceeded to purge all lower-level cadres whose loyalty he suspected. From then on, the Southwest Zone remained a firm power base for the radical-nationalist faction in the CPK.

From 1973, even harsher policies were introduced by the Khmer Rouge in an effort to mobilize the rural population. A large-scale programme was begun to relocate whole villages to new sites where everyone lived and worked communally. No private property was allowed, hours of work were long, and all former customs, including the practice of Buddhism, were prohibited. The effect was completely to disorientate people by severing their cultural roots and destroying their traditional lifestyles. But productivity increased as people were forced to work longer and harder. For both reasons, relocation was a technique increasingly favoured by the Khmer Rouge. In some areas in 1973 it was used to destroy pro-Vietnamese influence, by breaking up cells and networks established by the Khmer Vietminh, disrupting social relations, and placing the population at the mercy of the CPK's tough and dedicated young peasant cadres.

By the time the Lon Nol regime surrendered in April 1975, the Communist Party of Kampuchea had extended its control throughout the country. Not that it was a united country, or a united Party. Angkar was supreme, but not monolithic. During the war, real political power had rested with the Party Committees in each of the five zones into which the country was then divided. Each Zone Committee was responsible for formulating and implementing local policy decisions, and for conscripting, training, and committing the Zone armed forces. This regional autonomy meant that local Khmer Rouge commanders had amassed considerable personal authority which they were loath to surrender. Party instructions were interpreted by officials at all levels as they saw fit, and variation from region to region was considerable.

In April 1975 the Party Central Committee was faced with the task of extending its authority throughout the country. The common experience of war and revolution had given the CPK a sense of unity which carried over into the immediate postwar period. However, this tenuous unity proved unable to withstand the factional differences which soon became evident within the Party. During the war there had been broad agreement on both programme and priorities. The war came first, together with a determination to prevent any other political group from sharing power, either the Khmer Vietminh, or the Sihanoukists. Also a broad consensus had developed which saw Vietnam and Vietnamese designs for Indochina as a long-term threat to the independence of the Kampuchean people and their revolution. A united, powerful socialist Vietnam was seen as a greater menace to the sovereignty of Kampuchea even than Western imperialism. Disagreement remained, however, on how the Vietnamese threat should be countered, and on how relations between Kampuchea and Vietnam as two neighbouring communist states should be conducted.

These differences were present at the highest levels within the Party on the eve of victory. At the time, however, they did not seem too important, and majority decisions were accepted as binding. But in retrospect, in the disagreements which came to light at this time lay the seeds of later factional strife leading to the attempted coups and purges which tore the CPK apart in 1977 and 1978.

According to later evidence, a "Special Centre Assembly" was held on 17 April 1975, the day Phnom Penh was liberated, which brought together the full Central Committee and all Zone and Region secretaries of the CPK. In his address to the Assembly, Pol Pot reportedly called for the immediate application of an eight-point action programme, as follows:

1. Evacuate people from all towns.
2. Abolish all markets.
3. Withdraw the Lon Nol currency, but withhold the revolutionary currency which had been printed.
4. Defrock all Buddhist monks, and put them to work growing rice.
5. Execute all leaders of the Lon Nol regime, beginning with the top leaders.
6. Establish high-level cooperatives throughout the country, with communal eating.
7. Expel the entire Vietnamese minority population.

8. Despatch troops to the country's borders, particularly the border with Vietnam.

Considerable debate took place over a number of these points. Some speakers foresaw difficulties in immediately forming high-level cooperatives, given the need to absorb more than three million city dwellers who had no previous experience of revolutionary politics or communal living or working. Others doubted whether markets and money could be suddenly abolished without any preparation or warning. And some disagreed with the policy of execution instead of the usual communist practice of political re-education in labour camps. But there seems to have been general agreement over the other points: evacuation of the cities, expulsion of the Vietnamese, abolition of the Buddhist monastic order, and defence of the frontiers of the state.[13] Eventually the entire programme was adopted; but not before the extent of opposition by those favouring a more gradual approach to socialist transformation, and a less belligerent attitude towards Vietnam had convinced the radicals that some of their comrades were not sufficiently vigorous in their revolutionary commitment, and not to be trusted.

The degree of regional autonomy still existing in the CPK meant that some aspects of the programme were put into effect more or less gradually, or with more or less leniency in different areas. For example, though markets were immediately abolished and no new currency circulated, private barter and the use of gold as a medium of exchange was more firmly suppressed in some regions than in others. So, too, the policy of execution of all Lon Nol officers and officials was pursued more vigorously in some regions than in others, at least at first; and the introduction of high-level cooperatives and communal eating was delayed in some areas for months after being introduced elsewhere.

Other policies were more uniformly and enthusiatically pursued. The evacuation of the cities left them like ghost towns, eerie and lifeless. Phnom Penh was reduced to the vestige of a city, inhabited by a few trusted cadres, officials and troops. When Sihanouk returned to Phnom Penh in September 1975, he and his retinue estimated the total population at no more than 50,000.

The expulsion of the Vietnamese minority in Kampuchea was equally thorough. Convoys of barges were sent up the Mekong from southern Vietnam to transport evacuees. Many left by road. Those who stayed were mostly married to Cambodians, and considered themselves assimilated. This did not save them later when hostilities broke out between Democratic Kampuchea and Vietnam. Most were then massacred, often together with their spouses and children — in order to rid the state of traitors, and to preserve the purity of the Khmer race!

The Khmer also acted in a concerted fashion against Buddhism. Monks in Phnom Penh were ordered out of their pagodas along with the rest of the population. Some elderly monks, including Samdech Sangh Huot That, patriarch of the majority Mahanikai sect, who elected to remain, are reported to have been executed. But though almost everywhere monks were forced to return to lay life, only a few leading monks were killed in 1975. This was sufficient, however, to destroy the monastic order, the *Sangha*, as an organization with stong moral influence in Khmer society. In some places monks continued to live and work together at farming or irrigation projects: elsewhere former monks were reintegrated with the local population. Quite a number of Khmer Rouge cadres were themselves former monks.

The new regime moved quickly to seal the borders of the country, particularly with Vietnam and Thailand. Khmer Rouge troops reached the border town of Poipet within days of the surrender of Phnom Penh, but not before thousands of Khmer refugees from western Kampuchea had fled into Thailand. The presence of Khmer Rouge troops along the disputed border with Vietnam led to a number of frontier skirmishes, especially in the so-called Parrot's Beak area of Svay Rieng province that thrusts to within sixty kilometres of Saigon. Scattered fighting took place throughout 1975 at various points along the frontier from Kompong Cham in the north to Kampot in the extreme south. Fighting also took place on two disputed coastal islands. Relations with Vietnam thus got off to a bad start, though incidents decreased in 1976 when agreement was reached on the need to demarcate the common border between the two states. But 1976 marked no more than a lull in the fighting. Renewed outbreaks of border warfare the following year led to a break in diplomatic relations between the two countries and this set the stage for the eventual Vietnamese invasion which toppled the Khmer Rouge regime.

In 1975, however, factional differences which already existed within the Party were well hidden. In the eyes of the mass of the population Angkar was monolithic and all-powerful. Its mysterious secret workings revealed none of its internal weaknesses. These became evident only later, even to many within the Party, as contradictions in internal and foreign policies became more apparent. People like Bunheang Ung knew nothing of factions or policy differences. Angkar for them was the entire organizational structure of the Party, comprising every cadre and every soldier who had fought for the revolution. At another level Angkar referred to the central policy-making apparatus, the unknown membership of the Central Committee and its Secretariat, and ultimately the all-powerful Politburo. There a tiny group held power, most of them French-educated teachers and intellectuals. They included Pol Pot, Ieng Sary, Nuon Chea, Son Sen, and Vorn Veth. Khieu Samphan was not a member of the Politburo. Nor were other such leading figures in the Party as Non Suon and Hu Nim, both of whom held ministerial rank in the new government. But few of these men were even known by name to those they ruled. Although the CPK had announced its existence and leadership of the armed struggle at the end of September 1972, membership of the party was still secret. For everyone, those from the "liberated zones" and evacuees from Phnom Penh alike, all identities were hidden behind the impersonal mask of Angkar, the organization whose power was henceforth to direct the lives of every Kampuchean.

CHAPTER 3

Maesor Prachan

None of the evacuees from the city had any idea of what the future might hold as they made their way slowly towards their native villages, or settled down where Khmer Rouge cadres or village officials permitted them to stay.[1] Only gradually did the full extent of the social transformation undertaken by Angkar become apparent. But by the time the Ung family reached Maesor Prachan some things were already obvious. Life would be hard, they would have to grow their own food, and they would have to be careful with the new authorities. The young cadres of the Khmer Rouge held a power over life and death against which there was no appeal. Resistance would be punished. But despite this they still held some hope for the future. Once the new regime settled down, once hard work had produced from the fertile soil of Kampuchea the usual surplus of food; then there would be a need for educated and professional men, for engineers and scientists to build the new state; then they would return to Phnom Penh to offer their services and have their abilities recognized.

The Ung family reached Maesor Prachan in the middle of May. The village had a population of around 12,000, a figure swollen by the influx of evacuees. It comprised a group of seven hamlets (phum), roughly similar in population, strung out along the Tonle Toch waterway. Each hamlet consisted of sturdy wooden houses on stilts, with tiled or thatched roofs, set around with papayas, bananas, mango trees, and sugar palms. Behind the village stretched away the rich, irrigated rice lands of the lower Mekong, their fertility replenished by the annual monsoon floods. The village lay about forty kilometres northeast of Phnom Penh, and about twice that distance west of the Vietnamese border. It differed little from hundreds of other similar villages in that part of Prey Veng province, now renamed Region (damban) 22 of the Eastern Zone by the Khmer Rouge.

Many of Bun's relatives who had remained in Maesor Prachan lived in the principal hamlet, Phum Maesor Prachan. There Bun and his immediate family went to stay with his father's cousin. But on the orders of the Khmer Rouge village chief, Bun's family was assigned to live in Phum Andong together with the family of one of his uncles. Another uncle was assigned to Phum Memol hamlet, while his grandparents were sent to Phum Yot. The extended family was thus broken up and separated, a usual policy under the Khmer Rouge.

For three weeks Bun and his family camped in the grounds of the Phum Andong Buddhist pagoda while Bun and Kylin Chy, his brother-in-law, constructed their own house. The hamlet chief of Phum Andong showed them where they were to build, on a small patch of land close to the house of a long-time resident of the village. All evacuees were assigned land this way, dispersed throughout the hamlet so that they could be placed under the surveillance of the old inhabitants.

An old man named Leng, a former carpenter who had been a close friend of Bun's grandfather, helped them construct their house. It was simply made of bamboo and palm thatch and took little more than a week to complete because, unlike the traditional houses, it was constructed on the ground with a floor of stamped earth. Some building materials were provided, but not enough; additional materials had to be purchased by barter from people living in the hamlet (since by then all currency had been withdrawn). To obtain what they needed, evacuees had to exchange clothing, personal belongings, or a little of the gold or silver they had managed to smuggle past Khmer Rouge check points during their evacuation. The floor area of the Ung's house measured approximately three-by-five metres. Inside one corner was curtained off for Kim An and Kylin, and most of the remaining space was taken up by beds for the rest of the family. A small kitchen projected from the rear of the house.

While living in the pagoda, every member of the family had to write out his or her personal history, stating who they were,

Map of Maesor Prachan

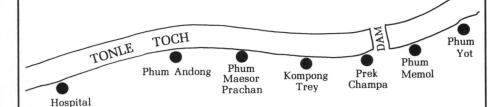

TONLE TOCH

DAM

Hospital

Phum Andong

Phum
Maesor
Prachan

Kompong
Trey

Prek
Champa

Phum
Memol

Phum
Yot

MAESOR PRACHAN

PEAREANG DISTRICT

Snaypol

Gaol

Karathann

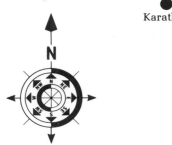

Inside Bun's family quarters.

Writing out personal histories.

past activities, and what they had done during the period of the Lon Nol regime. After these had been completed to the satisfaction of the authorities, the family was permitted to move into its new home.

It was not what Bun had been used to. His grandfather Polay Ung, and grandmother, Neang Sar, had left Maesor Prachan more than thirty years before, during the unsettled period of World War II and the Japanese occupation. Already at that time the Khmer Issarak were active in the area. Polay Ung moved to Phnom Penh, and when the war ended he decided to stay. Of his four grown sons, one obtained a degree in pharmacy from the University of Montreal, while the other three, including Bun's father, became private contractors, builders, and entrepreneurs.

In 1947 Bun's father Khunmeng Ung, went to Battambang in the northeast of Kampuchea, where he set up business as a supply contractor for the provincial authorities. There he met and married Bun's mother, Tanhay. Before long he was overseeing construction in a number of other provincial centres as well as Phnom Penh. In 1965 the family moved to the capital permanently, but three years later Khunmeng Ung was forced to retire through ill health. He died in 1971, leaving the family in a comfortable house on Sihanouk Avenue (renamed 18 March Road by Lon Nol in commemoration of his coup). Bun was born in Battambang in May 1952, third of a family of six children. His elder sister, Kim An, studied chemistry and later married Kylin Chy, a young engineer in food technology. Bun's elder brother, Bun An, won a Colombo Plan scholarship in 1970 to study in Australia, where he took a Bachelor of Economics degree, followed by a Master of Business Administration. He was still overseas when the Lon Nol government surrendered and remained in Australia throughout the period of Pol Pot's ascendency. This left Bun as the oldest son, with the responsibility of looking after his mother, two younger sisters and his younger brother, Bunthieng, then aged seven.

Bun himself went to primary school in Battambang until 1964, when he entered the Fine Arts High School in Phnom Penh. In addition to Kampuchean language and literature, maths and general science, students studied the history of art, painting, sculpture, traditional arts and crafts, and industrial design. Four teachers in painting and three sculptors were Russians. (At the time relations between Kampuchea and the United States had become strained to the point of rupture.) Bun remembered his Russian teachers with affection. They spoke no Kampuchean, and worked through interpreters, but they were competent and enthusiastic. Dimitri, a cartoonist from Leningrad, made a particular impression on Bun, and did more than anyone else to shape his subseqent career as a cartoonist and animator. After matriculating in 1972, Bun continued his studies at the University of Fine Arts, a continuation of the School at the tertiary level. He was within a few months of graduating when the Lon Nol government collapsed.

The village of Maesor Prachan was governed by a committee (kanak) of five: the village chief who was responsible for transmitting official policy and day-to-day administration; his deputy in charge of economic matters; a member in charge of security; a member to look after social welfare and health; and a member whose task it was to promote a new socialist culture, and to stamp out all vestiges of the decadent culture and morality of the former regime. Each hamlet was similarly administered by a five-man committee whose members had identical tasks. In Phum Maesor Prachan the hamlet chief was a man named Eak, half Kampuchean and half Chinese. He was the first Khmer Rouge official with whom Bun had any dealings and, though strict, seemed sympathetic to the plight of the evacuees.

The hamlet chief of Phum Andong was a former monk called Yon, a short, swarthy man with thick curly hair, a native of the hamlet who had joined the Khmer Rouge during the war against Lon Nol. Bun remembered Yon as a hard, but not a cruel man. His deputy at the time of Bun's arrival was Heng and the security chief was Sok, both later replaced. While the Ung family had little to do with Heng, Sok managed to make their lives a misery. He was brutal in his dealings with evacuees, and constantly on the lookout for any criticism of the new regime. Any such criticism was punished by arrest and interrogation. Anyone considered guilty could be sent to the district prison for "re-education" (rean saut) from which no-one ever returned. Everyone feared Sok's spies.

For purposes of administration and the organization of labour, the people of Phum Andong were divided into five groups, each numbering between 200 and 400 men, women and children. Each group had its own chief, responsible to the hamlet committee, though these were frequently changed. Roughly the population of the hamlet was made up of two-thirds "old people" (pracheachon chas), also known as "base people" who had lived continuously in the "liberated zone" with the Khmer Rouge, and one-third "new people" (pracheachon thmey), or "17 April people" who had remained in, or fled to, areas under control of the Lon Nol government. The two groups were treated very differently by the Khmer Rouge, no matter what the class origins of the "new people". In fact the "new people" constituted a class of their own. In a very real sense, they were considered as prisoners of war, potential enemies still committed to the old order who would, if the opportunity offered, sabotage attempts to construct the new Kampuchea. "Old people" were warned to be suspicious of the "new people", and to supervise their activities at all times.

The Khmer Rouge had first come to Maesor Prachan in 1970, soon after the overthrow of Sihanouk. But the village did not fall within the liberated zone until 1973. Before that, Maesor Prachan lay in disputed territory, competed for by both government forces and the guerrillas. Even after 1973, the harsh recruitment methods applied elsewhere were never enforced in the village; nor had the more rigorous techniques of population control, including the forced relocation of whole populations, been put into effect. Not surprisingly, therefore, many "old people" in the village were well disposed towards the Khmer Rouge. They accepted Khmer Rouge promises at face value; they looked forward to building a new Kampuchea; and they believed that the only thing that could prevent the dawning of a new age was lack of cooperation on the part of the "new people".

In part these attitudes were shared by Bun's relatives. Some members of his extended family, the descendants of his grandfather's brothers, refused to talk to Bun at all because he was a "new person". They apparently wanted thereby to convince the village leadership of their commitment to the new regime. Two of his father's cousins were Khmer Rouge cadres. Merely to have relatives who were "new people" was a disadvantage for them, one which other, poorer peasants did not suffer. Bun believed there was another, more personal reason why the Ung family relatives did not welcome them, and that was personal jealousy. His second cousins of about his own age were envious of the opportunities Bun had had, of his education and artistic talent, and yet scornful of them as being valueless for the only thing that counted in the new Kampuchea — physical labour in the fields. In the time that he stayed in Maesor Prachan, Bun did not become close to any of his cousins. Only some of his older relatives confided to him, privately when they chanced to be alone, how they hated the Khmer Rouge!

As much as possible the city ('new') people and country ('old') people were segregated from each other at the social level. "New people" with relatives in the village did not move in and live with them, or even live nearby: they had to construct houses where they were told, where someone to whom they were not related could keep an eye on them. The two groups did not mix easily in their everyday activities. Only in their formal work details did the two groups come together, again mainly to enable the "old people" to supervise the "new" and report any slackening of effort or complaints against the regime.

Only "new people" had to attend the frequent consciousness-building (kosang) sessions. At first these consisted of instruction by the hamlet chief, or a member of the hamlet committee, on the nature and objectives of the Kampuchean revolution. Information provided was simplistic and repetitive. The "new people" sat cross-legged on the floor, trying not to doze or look bored, under the watchful eyes of the hamlet committee, while Yon, the hamlet chief, criticized the former regime and all who, actively or unthinkingly, had supported it. Criticism centred on the traitorous reliance of the Lon Nol government on American imperialism, and particularly on the corrupting influence of Western capitalist culture and its selfish, individualistic values. "New people", Yon told them, never thought of the suffering of the poor. They exploited the labour of the poor for their own benefit. Now they had to think first of the interests of the people. Private property could only be accumulated at the expense of those who had little or nothing. There would be no private property in the new Kampuchea. They should forget their former existence, forget their houses in the city, their cars and television sets and household appliances. But they should never forget their crimes, their crimes against the people. By supporting the Lon Nol traitors, if only passively, they had failed to support the revolution. They had not fought for the people against American imperialism, and so they stood guilty in the eyes of the people. For those crimes they had to pay, by devoting themselves wholeheartedly to the cause of the revolution, by working for it to the maximum of their ability, by loving Angkar and obeying its commands. No opposition to the revolution would be tolerated. All had to obey the new revolutionary laws which governed the state, or risk the punishment of re-education.

Early consciousness-building sessions consisted of diatribes lasting hours at a time during which the same slogans and arguments were ceaselessly repeated. No discussion was permitted; no alternative view could be put. Later, self-criticism was introduced. "New people" were forced publicly to detail the sins they had committed, sins of omission as well as those of commission. Very little detail was given in these sessions on the future of the new Kampuchea. Everyone was told simply that they must work hard, produce more, and love Angkar. "If you believe in Angkar, you will live: if not, you will die", Yon told them.

People were given very little idea of national policies or programmes; and the village cadres themselves knew no more. They were told only what they were expected to do in their own area — construct new rice paddies, dig irrigation canals, plant crops. Marxism was initially never mentioned. Later, on occasions, one or another speaker would refer to Marxism-Leninism, but most people did not understand what the words meant. Nor could the crude and uneducated village cadres explain what Marxism-Leninism taught except in familiar, repetitive terms: concern for the masses, support for the revolution. At no time were translations of Marxist classics made available for study, and no Marxist texts were ever discussed. This was a Kampuchean revolution: the decisions of its own leaders alone constituted a suitable guide for the nation. Nothing else counted. As the cadres frequently told them, all they had to do was to work, eat and sleep. Angkar would do all their thinking for them.

All the "new people" were formally "invited" to join the hamlet cooperative (sahakor). Each of the five groups (krom) which made up the Phum Andong cooperative was further broken down into segregated sections with about twelve persons in each. Younger men, married or unmarried were organized into their own section; young women and younger married women formed another section. Together these two were known as the First Force (Kamlang timoui). Old men, old women, and children were each grouped into sections of their own. Each section had its leader who was responsible to the group leader.

The five groups in Phum Andong were of variable size, as were the sections, which constituted the smallest unit of cooperative labour. Everyone in the section was responsible for the enthusiasm and vigour with which other members worked. All sections included both "new" and "old" people, with the latter in the majority. "Old" people were expected to tell the "new people" what to do and to teach them their peasant skills. "New people" could not be section leaders, and had to behave in a humble and obedient manner towards their revolutionary superiors. In 1975 cooperative work in the fields lasted from 6 to 11 a.m., then two hours off for lunch and a rest, and 1 to 5 p.m.. One day in ten was a holiday.

The first priority for the Ung family after completing their house was to plant a garden. A small ration of rice was distributed to each new family, but all other food had either to be grown or caught (fish were plentiful in the rivers and paddies), or bargained for from those who had any to spare. One *damloeung* of gold (about 37 grams) would buy 90 kilograms of rice or 20 kilograms of salt. A Japanese or Swiss watch could be exchanged for 60 kilograms of rice. A few small fish were also sometimes distributed when the group organized the men's section to go fishing; but people could also fish in their spare time. Bun became quite expert at setting a gill net. The Ung family planted their own vegetables, bananas, and papayas; and bartered clothing for a few chickens. The chickens were kept for eggs: like a good Buddhist, Bun's mother did not kill chickens for eating. Mostly in those early days the family ate boiled rice and a soup made from slices of banana stem and a green water vegetable, known as *tracuon*.

Every family was expected to be all but self-sufficient in providing not only their own food, but also their other needs. As the Khmer Rouge repeatedly told them, they had to be masters of their environment. This meant they had to make their own fish oil and palm-leaf torches for lighting (though sometimes a little poor quality kerosene was made available), collect their own wood for cooking, make fish nets and traps, grow and cure their own tobacco, and sew their own clothes. Women were expected to weave mats for floors and walls. Sugar was also made locally, by slowly boiling the tapped juice of the sugar palm. However, sugar was considered a luxury and its production and processing was the preserve of the "old people". "New people" were forbidden to go near the pots where the palm juice was being boiled down, though the place was a favourite with the village children who sometimes managed to steal a little while working. Sugar could be bartered at four times the rate of rice on the black market.

As soon as his house was built, Bun was assigned to the men's section, employed mostly in repairing paddy dykes by scooping up mud with his bare hands. In Kampuchea the rainy season comes in May and June, and it was essential to plant out seedlings of the wet season crop known as "heavy" rice. By July or August the harvest of dry season or "light" rice was brought in, providing the village with just enough rice to tide it over while the slower-growing wet season rice was maturing. For Bun the work was heavy and tiring. He had never had to labour so long and so hard. And yet in comparison with the stepped-up work programmes introduced in 1977 and 1978, it was not too onerous, just dirty and monotonous. No attempt was made to discover if any of the "new people" had skills which could be applied in the

Supplementing the rice diet.

"New" and "old" people perform allotted tasks.

village: they were there not to teach, but to learn, to be reformed by the "old people" through manual labour.

There was always the hope in the early days of the revolution that sooner or later evacuees would be allowed to return to Phnom Penh. Once they had proved their commitment to the revolution through enthusiastically working without complaint, once they were reformed, once the regime realized the need for educated men to run the complex economy of a modern state, then they believed they would be recalled, and their skills put to real use. In the meantime, patience and self-control . . .

In many parts of the country it was believed that the signal for a change of policy would be given by Sihanouk when he returned from Beijing to head the new regime. Then all would be well. The educated would be recalled to Phnom Penh.[2] But unbeknown to the evacuees, when Sihanouk did return to Phnom Penh in September 1975, it was to become a prisoner in his own palace. On 4 April 1976, he resigned as Head of State to make way for the new government of Democratic Kampuchea.

Rumours also circulated in Maesor Prachan of scattered resistance to the regime. In the early months people occasionally passed through the village, searching for missing relatives. They brought news from other areas which was eagerly seized upon by the "new people" to be discussed, elaborated upon, and passed on. But after the Khmer Rouge enforced restrictions on personal movement, even this source of information dried up.

The actual ploughing and preparation of the paddies was done by "old people", as only they knew how to drive the oxen and buffalo. "New people" were responsible for digging irrigation trenches, and for carrying the heavy bundles of rice seedlings from the village seed beds to the fields, for the women to plant out. "New people" had to work especially hard, in order to prove they were not lazy and that they were eager to work for the new regime. Immediately after work the leader of each section called section members together for a meeting to discuss the day's work, criticize shortcomings or poor performance, and determine how to do better. Meetings were held even in the rain. Each day a roll call was taken of all who had worked, to serve as the basis for the monthly rice distribution. Those who worked received 600 grams of unmilled rice a day; elderly people who performed no productive work (old women looked after the small children while their parents were in the fields) received 400 grams, and those who were unable to work (the sick) received 200 grams. Though not overly generous, these were liberal rations compared to other parts of the country. Those who did not work, and who were considered not to be really sick, got nothing. Everyone had to work to eat in the new Kampuchea. Children received proportionally less than adults, depending on their age. At the end of the month work points were calculated for each family. The group leader summoned the head of each family to receive the family ration — "old people" first. Each family had then to make their rice last until the next distribution.

Cooperative labour was used to grow crops of maize, bananas and cotton, as well as rice. Work was directed by the hamlet committees. Only after 5 p.m. were people free to work in their own gardens, to fish, or to gather water plants as green vegetables. At certain seasons, frogs, snails, crickets and some kinds of beetle could also be collected to be eaten as a delicacy in soup or with rice. For "new people", however, consciousness-building meetings took much of their spare time, and prevented them from augmenting their food supplies effectively. At these sessions "new people" were constantly urged to work harder, to struggle to understand and support the revolution. Those who had been wealthy, who were educated — "intellectuals", a category into which Bun fell — or who were fat and flabby were particular targets.

During this time and later, Bun knew nothing of events in the outside world. He could obtain no batteries for his little radio, and it was dangerous to ask questions. The Khmer Rouge listened only to Radio Phnom Penh, but international news was minimal. It was as if the rest of the world had ceased to exist. The only contact the village had with the wider world beyond its own limits was when Khmer Rouge cadres came from Snaypol, the administrative headquarters of Peareang district, to confer with village officials, inspect work sites, check on production targets, or sometimes to arrest someone. No "new people" dared speak to them, and they seldom volunteered any information. It was not even known what happened to those arrested. All that was known was that they were taken first to the district gaol (formerly the local high school on the outskirts of Snaypol) for questioning. What happened to them after that no-one knew, though it was assumed that they were sent to special camps to be re-educated.

In the first few months after Bun arrived in Maesor Prachan, a number of people were arrested and sent for re-education. All former Lon Nol officers had been "invited" by the village committee to present themselves at the pagoda in Phum Maesor Prachan for a meeting not long after Bun's arrival. Since everyone knew them in the village, most had made no attempt to

Section leaders criticize productivity of the day's work.

Former Lon Nol officers shown the graves of Khmer Rouge troops.

hide their identitities. When they assembled, about twenty of them, they were shown a cemetery behind the pagoda containing some forty graves. "These were comrades of ours who were killed by you", the Khmer Rouge told them. A few days later the Khmer Rouge "invited" them to report for re-education in Snaypol. All did so, including a cousin of Bun's who had been a captain in the Navy. As a student he had spent a year in Australia under the Colombo Plan, before joining the navy as an accountant in the pay corps. Not one who reported for re-education returned to the village or was ever seen again. All are now assumed to have been executed, but at the time the Khmer Rouge were taken at their word and it was generally believed that they were actually undergoing re-education.

Just the threat of re-education was enough to keep the population in line, for it meant at the very least a separation of unknown duration from one's family, the only remaining source of security for the disoriented evacuees. The village and hamlet cadres thus exercised extraordinary power, for in Maesor Prachan they *were* Angkar. Any orders they gave were immediately obeyed. Not to do so was to risk being accused of trying to sabotage the revolution. Formerly Buddhist monks had been the most respected members of the community, but their influence was moral, and exercised indirectly. Now the cadres ruled, but their power was based on coercion and fear. When Bun arrived in the village there were still three monks in Phum Andong pagoda. Soon after they were ordered to leave the *Sangha* and get married, which they did, even one old monk who had lived in the pagoda all his life and had been a friend of Bun's father. Not to have done so would have been to risk re-education.

It did not take the "new people" of Maesor Prachan long to learn to "love Angkar without limit", to work for Angkar, to accept without question the directives of Angkar. Perfect obedience was demanded. People were told to model themselves on the buffalo which worked without complaint at any time. The "Organization" constituted an authority that was answerable to no-one, for it held a complete monopoly of power. Even though in a village of 12,000 people it was represented by fewer than fifty cadres, its authority was absolute, for it ruled through fear. Fortunately for the Ung family, however, the power of Angkar was not too oppressive during 1975, thanks to the relatively benign conditions existing in the Eastern Zone. In other parts of Kampuchea, Angkar imposed a tyranny that was far more flagrant and oppressive.

CHAPTER 4

Learning to Live with the Khmer Rouge

All revolutionary laws and regulations were promulgated in the name of Angkar; all transgressions were known to and were punished by Angkar. Angkar was everywhere, a pervasive presence that none could escape. "Angkar has more eyes than a pineapple", the cadres said. Husbands and wives spoke of Angkar only in private, in a whisper, fearful of being overheard. No-one criticized Angkar in public; even the most minimally critical passing allusion could be enough to ensure arrest, interrogation, and subsequent disappearance for re-education. Danger was ever present; at no time did one know whether the spies of Angkar were listening.

Spies (chlop) were recruited by the security chief in every village and hamlet under the Khmer Rouge. Most who reported on a regular basis were teenage boys, but young girls and children under ten years old were also encouraged to inform on parents and friends. The identity of the official spies was usually known to people in the village, and they were both feared and loathed. Their job was to gather whatever information they could, by whatever means, about every member of the village. More especially, however, their targets were "new people". Spies sought information on the backgrounds of "new people" before they arrived in the village, and on their attitudes towards the regime. They snooped around at night attempting to overhear conversations or domestic arguments that would give away someone's identity. The *chlops* also tried to get the relatives of those they suspected to spy for them. Because no-one knew for certain that someone else would not inform on them, distrust became endemic, particularly between "new" and "old" people.

The identity of hamlet spies in Phum Andong was usually obvious because of their relation to Sok, the security chief. Whenever any youth was seen often with Sok and was clearly on good terms with him, he was taken to be a spy. But there were other spies in the village whose identity was secret. These reported not to the hamlet authorities, but to the village committee or the district *(srok)* security chief. Such spies reported less frequently, when they had important information to impart, and they did so in private, far from the watching eyes of the people of Phum Andong. Some were relatives of district-level Khmer Rouge cadres; others were friends. All were recruited secretly, unbeknown to the hamlet cadres, for one of their principal tasks was to spy on the hamlet cadres themselves — to report any failure to implement district directives, or any abuses of authority. The second hamlet chief of Phum Andong was arrested and executed because he tried to cover up the rape of a Chinese woman by two of his spies. He was denounced by a district spy.

The Kampuchean people are naturally reticent. They do not reveal their opinions readily to strangers. Under the Khmer Rouge, they learned to hide them from their friends. In Maesor Prachan, Bun and his family learned early to keep their thoughts to themselves, and especially not to speak in the presence of "old people", even their own relatives. "Old people" were all too ready to inform on the attitudes of "new people", and were on the look out for any slackening in resolute support for the revolution. Any stranger passing might overhear a snatch of conversation, and report it to the hamlet or village authorities. Even "new people" might spy on each other in order to ingratiate themselves with their new rulers. The children of "old people" would creep under the houses of "new people" at night to listen to what was said, and even the children of "new people" were urged to inform on their parents. Bun's young brother was questioned about what family members had done in Phnom Penh, but he confirmed that Bun had been a student. It was safest to say nothing, even at night. The only time Bun thought it safe to speak his mind to one of his immediate family was by day, on an open path with no trees or bushes nearby, and a clear view in all directions.

Even implied criticism of the regime was often reported. For example, to exclaim "Oh I'm so tired! Why do we have to work so hard?'' could be taken both as criticism of Angkar's policies, and as indicating laziness and a lack of dedication to the revolution. In Maesor Prachan, official action was not usually taken on the basis of the first such report. But the speaker would be a marked man, and would be watched carefully. The Khmer Rouge believed comments like these, if made frequently enough to work mates, could undermine their will to work and cause dissension and unrest. Anyone reported on would become the object of further spying. Additional adverse reports would be communicated by the *chlop* to the village authorities, and might lead either to an indirect warning from a member of the hamlet committee, perhaps delivered to another member of the family, or to pointed criticism at a consciousness-building session. No official warning would be given, however, and when someone was arrested, he often had no idea what for.

Arrests were carried out by district-level security forces, acting on the authority of the district chief who in turn acted on reports from the village. Arrests were usually at night, and were not brutal during the first year in the Eastern Zone. Prisoners were not publicly beaten or tortured. A suspect would be invited to accompany a cadre to the pagoda. Only there would he be tied up and taken away. Later, however, arrests were carried out by day, and on at least two occasions which Bun witnessed in 1977 and 1978, people were tied up and beaten with gun butts and sticks in front of assembled villagers.

The strain of being constantly on one's guard was difficult to live with. In time Bun got to know who most of the spies were, who were most likely to report anything overheard to the village authorities, who were most fanatical in support of the revolution. He even learned the identities of one or two of the district spies. But sometimes he forgot himself momentarily. It was all too easy to comment in disgust, while working in an irrigation ditch: ''Oh this is filthy work! I'm sick of it!'' Once when he made this mistake, the response was immediate. A well-known toady of the hamlet committee turned on Bun immediately demanding, ''Why did you say that? Don't you like the revolution? Don't you like Angkar? Would you like to rebel against Angkar?'' After that he was more careful.

Through their spying and threats of punishment the Khmer Rouge enforced a strict moral code. All forms of gambling were forbidden, as was the consumption of alcohol and use of drugs. Rice was the staple food, and its distribution was carefully controlled. Any surplus went to feed the cadres and the army. It was strictly forbidden to ferment rice and distil the liquor to make the

A hamlet meeting called to administer justice.

traditional Kampuchean rice wine *(Sra sar)*, or make beer from palm juice *(tuk thnaut chou)*. Anyone caught brewing or drinking alcohol was warned to mend his ways. If he persisted he was sent to the district prison for re-education. The very word, *rean saut*, was enough to make people afraid, and everyone avoided using it — except for some "old people" who seemed to obtain positive pleasure at the effect the word had on "new people".

Stealing was a serious crime which was usually punished publicly. In one incident Bun witnessed, a man accused of stealing a stem of bananas was arrested by a security cadre and paraded through the village. A hamlet meeting was then called, to administer justice, at which attendance was compulsory. Everyone sat on the ground and listened as the hamlet chief explained how the crime had been committed. The accused made a full confession, admitting his guilt and promising never to steal again. As this was a first offence, the culprit was let off with a severe warning and ordered to make restitution.

Other crimes were not punished so lightly. Adultery, for example, was particularly frowned upon. Men and women were strictly segregated during working hours, and were discouraged even from talking to each other in the village. No physical contact, such as holding hands, was permitted in public, even between members of the same family. The Khmer Rouge even tried to discourage physical affection in private on the grounds that such behaviour was a carry over from the decadent lifestyle of the former regime: it was not revolutionary. As this sexual morality was increasingly enforced, husbands and wives even feared to show affection in their own homes, lest some spy should report them to the authorities. Punishment for sexual offences was increased after 1975: thereafter the culprit, or culprits where both were to blame, were sent to prison.

As most people were terrified of transgressing the rules on sexual morality in Maesor Prachan, it was more often those in authority who committed sexual offences. However, they had always to be careful, for fear one of the district spies would report them. Also anyone who had suffered in any way at the hands of the village authorities was only too ready to take revenge by reporting any clandestine affair involving Khmer Rouge officials. Pin Yathay relates the story of a woman caught by soldiers in the act of making love to a Khmer Rouge official at Veal Vong in Pursat province. Under interrogation she claimed to have had sexual relations with two other officials noted for their cruelty. All four were taken into the forest and killed. As the woman had been separated from her husband and had seen her son taken off to a youth brigade work camp, her implication of two more officials was interpreted as an act of revenge. For the "new people" she was "an authentic heroine of the passive resistance".[1]

A whole set of regulations curtailed personal freedom of movement in Maesor Prachan. "Old" and "new" people were discouraged from visiting each other socially, in the evenings after work. However, it was possible for "new people" to visit each other's houses in the same hamlet, though permission had to be requested to go anywhere beyond the hamlet limits. Even to visit a close relative in another hamlet of Maesor Prachan required permission from the hamlet chief, and a good reason had to be given. Depending on his mood the hamlet chief said simply "yes" or "no", and would enter into no discussion. Frequent visiting was discouraged. When Bun asked to visit his grandmother in the next hamlet when she was sick, he was allowed on the first occasion, but refused permission to take her some food a day or two later. The hamlet chief told him: "Your grandmother is alright. Don't worry about her. Angkar will look after her. I cannot give you permission to go again." When Bun himself fell sick and was admitted to the hospital in Phum Maesor Prachan, his aunt could visit him because she lived in the hamlet, but his mother found it very hard to get permission to come from the neighbouring hamlet of Phum Andong. Travel beyond the village was out of the question for "new people", though "old people" could obtain permission to visit other villages in Peareang district, or even the district capital of Snaypol. A written pass was required for any travel beyond the village limits.

All rules and regulations had to be quickly learned by the "new people" and warnings were not repeated. The Khmer Rouge cadres were strict, humourless, often brutal, but not entirely arbitrary in their treatment of the evacuees from Phnom Penh. They were responsible for applying Party decisions. Every so often village officials were summoned to the District Party office where they would be instructed by their superiors on the current political line. But this still left considerable room for personal interpretation. A hamlet chief could be more or less harsh in his administration; though he had always to guard against accusations of leniency, especially any suggestion that he might not be sufficiently hard on "new people".

During 1975 when Yon was hamlet chief of Phum Andong, the Khmer Rouge were relatively mild in their treatment of the newcomers. The first priority for the hamlet was to grow enough rice to feed its swollen population. The winter rice was planted out in July in paddies some distance from the village. The first limited harvest was of light rice from fields near the village and was gathered early in August 1975. Maesor Prachan lies in that area of Prey Veng province which is annually inundated by the summer monsoon floods pouring down the Mekong River and by August the water was already rising fast. The rice was left to the last moment to ripen, but had to be harvested before the paddies were too deeply flooded.

In Maesor Prachan harvesting was done quickly, with men and women working day and night. The women, particularly those from the city, were frightened at night up to their waists in water under the eerie light of palm-leaf flares. They were most afraid of the large leeches, thicker than a man's finger, which infested the paddies. Slimy and bloated, they dropped off when fully fed, leaving a trickle of blood. Another species of tiny leech was considered even more dangerous, for it could slip into a woman's vagina or up a man's penis. There it would remain for two or three days until it detached itself and could be flushed out. The pain could be excrutiating. Bun was lucky enough never to have suffered in this way, but a close friend did. Everyone was bitten by leeches at one time or another.

In the flooded paddies the bundles of cut rice stalks were collected by boat, and carried back to Maesor Prachan by buffalo, or on the heads of the women. Rice grains were separated from the stalk by hand — or by foot, since the usual method was to hold onto a kind of handrail and thresh the bundles of rice by stamping on them. The work was continuous, for everyone feared criticism from the Khmer Rouge cadres for slacking.

After the last grains were gathered, the "new people" were ordered to transport it by ox-cart to the village rice store. As a special punishment for the good life they had known in Phnom Penh during the war, they were made to pull the carts themselves, harnessed like buffalo — much to the amusement of the "old people". .Children hit the carters with sticks or threw pebbles as they would at oxen. "The buffalos have worked hard. They should be pitied and given a rest", the "old people" joked.

After the first harvest, a strict guard was maintained by the Khmer Rouge at the entrance to each hamlet to prevent any unauthorized trading of rice. Smuggling of rice was strictly forbidden. Each family had to husk their own rice by hand, as the village possessed no mill. The work took a long time, but had to be performed outside communal working hours. During the flood season, known as the "high water", the surrounding rice paddies were a sea isolating the hamlets. Travel was by boat. Communal

Harvesting at night, in leech-infested paddies.

One of the punishments meted out to "new people".

The pedal-powered irrigation system.

At school in Maesor Prachan.

labour continued, however. While the men carved and plaited bamboo to make fish traps, repaired houses, dug vegetable gardens, or planted banana trees, the women wove mats or cloth, made carrying baskets of bamboo lined with clay, or prepared thatch for the roof.

Even after the first harvest, food was scarce. The village population had increased greatly. There were not enough vegetables, and during the floods fish were difficult to catch. Traps and nets were more effective once the water level fell. In the meantime most meals consisted of rice gruel and banana stems, with occasionally an egg or a little fish mixed with it. By October the water level had fallen. Fish were more plentiful, but as the moisture in the soil dried out, the paddies had to be irrigated by means of a pedalled waterwheel. Men worked for three hours at a stretch, had fifteen minutes break, and then pedalled for another three hours. Bun pedalled along with the other men in his section, his legs aching, under the watchful eye of the section chief. The section had been assigned to irrigate paddies about four kilometres from Phum Andong. Food was either carried from the village, or prepared on the spot so as to save time, since the lunch break had by then been reduced to one hour, from midday to 1 p.m. The days were hot and monotonous, but there were few complaints. No-one dared to object. The Khmer Rouge told them: "If we could fight for the revolution, you can work a little in the sun."

Everyone had their work to do. Men, women and children were woken by a bell at 5 a.m., ate and joined their respective work groups. Men had to be at the irrigation sites by 6 a.m. Women worked in the gardens, or frightened birds in the rice paddies. Children from the ages of six to fifteen and the elderly had to clean the streets of the village and tidy their homes. Children collected cattle and buffalo dung to make manure for the gardens. Some old men looked after the village; others with particular skills, such as ironworking, laboured in communal workshops, where they passed on their knowledge to others, usually "old people": new people had to do hard physical labour.

At 7 a.m. the children went off to school, boys and girls each in their separate sections. The leaders of each section would be children of "old people", usually older children aged fourteen or fifteen. Sections were of mixed ages, which meant that the younger children of "new people" were often bullied and hit by older section leaders. When this happened no complaints were possible. New children were also victimized by the teachers who, despite the fact that most "new people" were better educated, were invariably "old people", often very poor peasants with a minimum of education and no training as teachers. In Phum Loeu the teachers used to beat the children of "new people" regularly, but in Phum Andong this did not occur.

The school in Phum Andong was in the buffalo stables. The buffalo were taken early to graze and the dung in the stables swept up before school began. Classes lasted until 11 a.m. when the children had two hours for lunch. Children were taught in four grades. They learned to read and write, though painfully slowly. Bun's little brother knew his letters, and could write his own name before the evacuation from Phnom Penh. After three and a half years of schooling in Phum Andong he had forgotten even that! The children had no pencils or books. They had to make their own chalk out of clay, and were given only waste paper from used cement bags to write on. Apart from some elementary arithmetic, most of the time was taken up by learning revolutionary songs, how to love Angkar, and in being indoctrinated into socialist morality. They were told again and again of the need to work hard, to protect the revolution by reporting on their parents and relatives, of the glories of Kampuchean socialism, and the danger posed by Vietnam.

In the afternoons the children worked, each in his or her section. They helped build small dykes in the vicinity of the hamlet, for paddies or vegetable gardens, watched over the cattle or buffalo as they grazed, or carried dung to the fields. In the three months of the year when there was no school they worked at the same kind of jobs all day, ran errands or helped adults. The Khmer Rouge told them: "In revolutionary Kampuchea, every day is a holiday!" In the evenings they helped their parents to prepare the meal, husked rice, or cared for their younger brothers or sisters. There was no time for play.

Once every three days all the men, women and children in the hamlet assembled separately for meetings known as *prachum chivapeap* (literally, "livelihood meeting"). Hamlet leaders talked about socialism, and Angkar, and the need for hard work. Men and women were criticized for being late for school or for work, for not having the right attitudes. Most criticism was directed against the "new people", especially those families from which a member had been sent for re-education.

Because of poor nutrition and hard physical labour to which they were unaccustomed, many "new people" fell sick at one time or another. At such times, although there was a hamlet committeeman in charge of health and social services, health care

After school.

was minimal. There was an almost complete lack of modern medicines, even of such basic drugs as aspirins and anti-malarial tablets. In 1975 it was still possible to obtain some kinds of medicine through barter on the black market, although few people would agree to part with what was for them a most precious possession. Later, drugs became almost impossible to procure. To make up for the lack of modern medicines, traditional remedies were resorted to. These included the use of certain leaves, roots and bark, which were said to be part of the ancient folk pharmacopoeia of the Khmer people. All were manufactured in the village in a room of the hospital. For example, a tonic made from ground bark mixed with milk was said to renew the strength of those recovering from illness. One kind of pill, still called "aspirin", was made by mixing lemon juice with manioc powder, and was considered by the "new people" to be quite valueless. Diarrhoea was treated with small black pills made from roots called "rabbit-droppings". The only pill which people liked was one for stomach disorders made of honey and manioc. Those who were sick and could ask for medicine at the village dispensary. Childbirth took place at home, the husband being given three days off work to look after his wife.

After the high water receded in 1975, Maesor Prachan was given an additional area of rice land to farm. The area formerly owned by the villagers was insufficient to support the increased population, and the additional manpower available needed to be productively employed. The new land was situated at Tuol Don Teov, some twenty kilometres east of Snaypol and over thirty-five kilometres from Maesor Prachan. As this was an impossibly long distance to walk every day the village authorities established a "work site" (karatan) where workers remained up to a fortnight at a time.

Everyone had to carry their own bed mats, blankets, mosquito nets, cooking and eating utensils, food, work tools, and even building materials to the site. So heavy were the loads that some girls were crying and collapsing with fatigue by the time they arrived. The first night they slept on the ground, and the next day constructed rough accommodation to house groups of workers: men in one place, women some distance away. At first each section cooked for itself, but as this took too much time and allowed time off in rotation for cooking, the Khmer Rouge soon introduced communal cooking and dining.

The principal task at the work site was literally to reshape the landscape. In this region, most peasants had previously owned their own land. A richer peasant often possessed a number of

The Khmer Rouge feast while villagers starve.

Hospital patients set to work during convalescence.

paddies some distance from each other. Some he rented to poorer peasants, others he worked himself. Paddies were subdivided by innumerable dykes of uneven shape. The Khmer Rouge decided to rationalize paddy size and shape by breaking down existing dykes and replacing them with new, geometrically precise ones around fields each 100 metres square. A large irrigation canal was dug around each area of one square kilometre. This was designed to destroy any basis for private ownership of land and no-one dared criticize even if his own family land was involved. Bun considered the new paddies a good idea: they looked more neat and attractive, especially when planted with young green rice. Also they were easier to irrigate, because they could be served by a better system of canals — although the water still had to be raised by pedalling the old irrigation wheels.

A few months after the work site was established, everyone was assembled to be told about the new constitution and elections for the Assembly of the People's Representatives of Kampuchea. The Constitution was decided upon at the Fourth National Congress of the CPK meeting in Phnom Penh in December 1975 and promulgated on 5 January 1976.[2] The Constitution was drawn up, as it stated, in accordance with "the fundamental and sacred aspirations of the industrial workers, peasants and other workers, and the soldiers and officers of the Revolutionary Army of Kampuchea", whose wish was

> to create an independent, united, peaceful, neutral, nonaligned Kampuchea sovereign in its territorial integrity, in a society where happiness, equality, justice, and genuine democracy reign, where there are neither rich nor poor people, neither oppressive nor oppressed classes, a society in which the whole people lives in harmony, in a framework of national unity, and joins their efforts in productive labour, to build and defend the country together.

The irony was not lost on Bun.

The Constitution was brief and simply worded. The article on the economy (Article II) stated only that: "All important means of production are the collective property of the people's State and of the people in common. Articles of everyday life remain in individual ownership." According to Article XII, "Every industrial worker is the master of his factory. Every peasant is the master of his rice fields, and land ... There is absolutely no unemployment in Democratic Kampuchea." The new culture of Democratic Kampuchea was "national, popular, progressive, and wholesome" in contrast to the "depraved and reactionary culture of the oppressive classes and of the forces of colonialism and imperialism in Kampuchea" (Article III).

Justice was said to be "exercised by the people", the major crimes being those "systematically hostile or destructive activities that endanger the people's State". Other crimes were to be dealt with through re-education (Article X). Polygamy and polyandry were specifically prohibited (Article XIV). So too was "any reactionary religion which threatens the interests of Kampuchea and its people" — this notwithstanding that "Every citizen of Kampuchea has the right to hold any faith or religion and also the right to hold no faith or religion" (Article XX). Every citizen had "the duty to defend and build the country in accordance with his means and his capacities" (Article XIV). But only "the sons and daughters of industrial workers, peasants, and other categories of workers" had the right to join one of the three categories of fighters (regular, regional or guerrilla) making up the Revolutionary Army (Article XIX). Finally, in foreign policy, great stress was placed on Kampuchean neutrality, and the government's refusal to permit any country whatever to establish military bases on its territory (Article XXI). Foreign interference in the nation's internal affairs was resolutely rejected "whether of military, political, cultural, economic, social, diplomatic, or of so-called humanitarian character" (Article XXI).

At the meeting on the Constitution held at Maesor Prachan no discussion was permitted. On 20 March 1976, more than 10,000 people, including inhabitants of other hamlets situated near the Tuol Don Teov work site, gathered to vote for the Assembly of the People's Representatives. The 250 member Assembly was to comprise 150 peasant representatives, 50 industrial workers, and 50 from the Revolutionary Army. No other classes existed in Democratic Kampuchea. Everyone sat in rows in the newly-constructed square paddies. Several speeches were made praising Khmer Rouge policies, then each person was given a piece of paper on which was written one name, that of the officially-selected candidate, Tum Choen. Voting consisted of rows of people in order filing past the voting box into which they placed the votes they had been given, all under the careful scrutiny of Khmer Rouge cadres. Bun's opinion, which he of course never expressed, was that this Assembly vote, which had to be performed "with a smiling face", was nothing but a "shameful farce".

On 14 April, Phnom Penh radio announced formation of a new Government of Democratic Kampuchea with Pol Pot as

Prime Minister. Other ministers included Ieng Sary (Foreign Affairs), Son Sen (Defence), Vorn Veth (Economy) and Hu Nim (Information). Khieu Samphan was named President of the National Praesidium with So Phim, the Eastern Zone Party Secretary, and Nhim Ros, Party Secretary of the Northwest Zone, as vice Presidents.[3] What was not evident to people in the villages was that the composition of the new government reflected a careful balance of ideological factions within the CPK, factions which, though they agreed on the need for the socialist transformation of Kampuchean society and on the seriousness of the threat posed by Vietnam, differed over the best tactics and strategies to employ in effecting that transformation and meeting that threat. As a result, in different parts of the country, policies were applied more or less harshly. The relatively benign conditions in the Eastern Zone were not experienced in the new villages of the north and northwest.

CHAPTER 5

The New Villages

The Ung family were lucky on two counts during 1975: they managed to return to their home village where they were known and had relatives and friends; and their village was in the Eastern Zone, where Khmer Rouge policies were implemented in a relatively benign way.[1] Many evacuees from Phnom Penh were forced to follow routes out of the city leading away from instead of towards their home provinces. Some were able to make their way in a broad arc back around Phnom Penh; but others, exhausted by the evacuation, settled down in the first village in which they were permitted to take refuge. Families with elderly relatives or very young children could not continue moving day after day. Some families had such tenuous ties to their places of origin that there seemed no good reason to trek perhaps hundreds of miles under appalling conditions (it was then the beginning of the rainy season) to a village where nobody remembered them. For those families who had lived for generations in Phnom Penh, including most of the capital's large Chinese minority, one village was as good as another. The Ung family may not have been made welcome by some of their relatives, but they had kept in contact with the village, and they were not among total strangers.

But more important, Maesor Prachan was in the Eastern Zone, the richest food-growing area (along with Battambang in

Elections in Democratic Kampuchea.

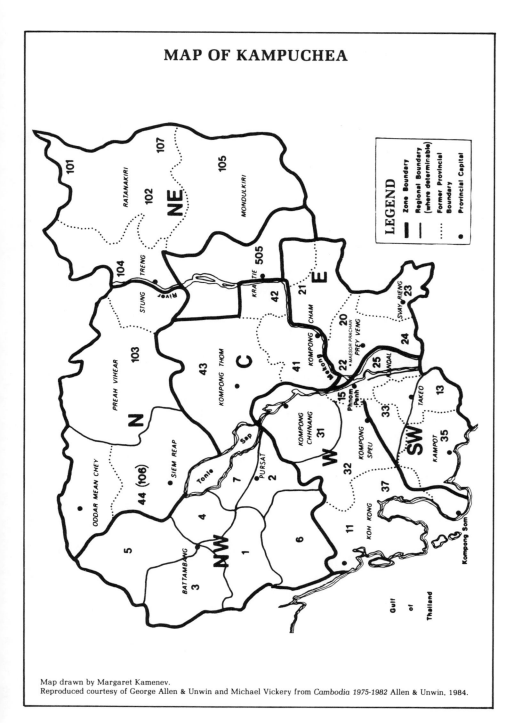

MAP OF KAMPUCHEA

101

107

RATANAKIRI

102

NE

105

MONDULKIRI

104

STUNG TRENG

River

505

KRATIE

42

21

E

KOMPONG CHAM

20

SVAY RIENG

23

PREAH VIHEAR

103

N

43

KOMPONG THOM

C

41

MAESOR PRACHAN

PREY VENG

22

24

25

ODDAR MEAN CHEY

SIEM REAP

44 (106)

5

Tonle

Sap

7

PURSAT

2

KOMPONG CHHNANG

31

W

15

Phnom
Penh

KOMPONG SPEU

33

SW

TAKEO

13

35

KAMPOT

32

4

NW

1

6

11

KOH KONG

37

Kompong Som

BATTAMBANG

3

Gulf
of
Thailand

Map drawn by Margaret Kamenev.
Reproduced courtesy of George Allen & Unwin and Michael Vickery from *Cambodia 1975-1982* Allen & Unwin, 1984.

the northwest) in Kampuchea. Because of the influx of evacuees, food was in short supply during 1975, but no-one starved in Maesor Prachan, or in other rice-growing areas of the region. Fish were plentiful and vegetables grew easily. Conditions were worse in those areas in the east where maize was grown, but even so, not as bad as in many other parts of the country. The favourable natural conditions and agricultural potential of the Eastern Zone were matched by the relatively moderate political line enforced there — moderate, that is, in comparison with other zones, particularly the North and Northwest, or with the harsher policies later enforced during 1977 and 1978.

Administratively, Democratic Kampuchea was divided into seven zones after 1975 — the Northeast, North, Northwest, West, Southwest, East and Centre. The Kratie Special Region (known as 505) separated the Northeast from the East and Centre, while a second Special Region (106) centred on Siem Reap close to the ruins of Angkor, was abolished in 1977 to be incorporated into the Northern Zone. A third smaller Special Region (15) surrounded the capital of Phnom Penh. Each Zone was divided into numbered regions of *dambans* (the five in the Eastern Zone were 20, 21, 22, 23 and 24). Regions were further divided into districts *(srok)*, each containing a number of large villages *(khum)* like Maesor Prachan composed of smaller hamlets *(phum)*.[2]

The East differed from other Zones in a number of important respects. For example, in the East, unlike most other areas, important "intellectuals" were separated from other evacuees and sent to construct special work camps. For the Khmer Rouge anyone who had completed a tertiary education was an intellectual. The category included doctors, engineers, pharmacists, teachers and even some students who had not yet graduated. Work camps of this kind were the closest thing in Kampuchea to the re-education camps established for military officers and civil servants of the former regimes in Laos and southern Vietnam. For the most part, however, little or no attempt was made to re-educate "new people" in the sense of convincing them of the historical necessity for, or social justice of, the revolution. They were enemies, incorrigible, and would remain so. Their only use to the regime was not in the application of their former skills, but in working as agricultural labourers. What political education there was took the form of endless repetition of simple slogans by often illiterate cadres. No questions and no discussion were permitted. Physical labour and agricultural production were all that mattered.

The East was different too in that no new villages were established there. Especially in the sparsely-populated areas of the North and Northwest, new villages were carved out of virgin forest or jungle as part of a plan to extend the total area under cultivation. Though they needed some support at first in the form of small rations of rice and a few simple tools, these new villages aimed to become first self-sufficient, and then to produce a surplus which would go to the state. The future for inhabitants of new villages was to spend the rest of their lives as the poorest of peasant farmers, their standard of living maintained by their masters at no more than a subsistence level.

Almost all new villages were established by evacuees from Phnom Penh or provincial towns. But many of the "new people" in these villages were not highly educated and had formerly been factory workers, petty traders, or low-level government servants such as soldiers, road workers, cleaners or clerks. In a few areas "old people" were also assigned to help establish these villages, though this was not usual. The usual pattern was to establish new villages in the forest beyond the limits of cultivation of an old village, thus giving "new people" an opportunity to trade with "old" ones in nearby villages to obtain a few necessities of life while working to establish their own village.

Life for those assigned to new villages was much harsher than for those integrated into old, established villages. Often people had to walk for days over muddy village tracks carrying all their belongings in order to reach the area of forest they were to clear. On arrival they were given a three or four day 'holiday' during which each family was expected to build a hut of bamboo, woven palm and thatch. Until a roof was constructed everyone slept in the open, sheltering during heavy showers as best they could under palm leaves or branches. Each family was allotted a tract of forest to clear, perhaps two or three hectares in extent, which the family was expected to farm. As most of the land was marginal and unsuitable for making rice paddies, crops such as maize, yams, sweet potatoes and cassava were usually planted, together with vegetables and tropical fruits such as papayas and bananas.

As most "new people" had no tools, except perhaps a machete or knife, and as Angkar often failed to provide any, people were forced to use sharpened sticks as the only tools with which to dig the soil. Terraces had to be constructed by hand. Because of the shortage of draught animals after the war, ploughs borrowed from a nearby village frequently had to be pulled by teams of men. As at Maesor Prachan, work began at 6

Establishing a new village.

a.m. and lasted until 5 p.m., with one or sometimes two hours off for lunch. For men and women from the city, unused to physical labour, the work was hard and tedious. But the need for food spurred them on. The only food provided by Angkar was an inadequate ration of rice, which varied from place to place and time to time, and a little salt. Usually it was unhusked paddy rice at a rate at first of about sixteen kilograms a month for adult workers (or about 300 grams of milled rice per day), just enough on which to survive. Children and old people received proportionally less. Towards the end of 1975 these rations were progressively reduced in some areas until they gave out altogether, and people received only a little rice bran to eat.

Food quickly became an obsession for everyone in the new villages. There was never enough and the usual meal consisted of thin rice gruel mixed with bits of cassava or maize, green bananas or even slices of banana stem, and any other vegetable or edible water plant that could be found. People living near a river or lake could obtain permission to fish, provided they could trade some possession with "old people" for a net or trap, or learn to make one themselves. After work, and on their one day off in ten, families went into the jungle to search for edible plants and roots. Snails, various insects, small lizards and land crabs were all eagerly caught and added to the soup. Those "new people" lucky enough to have clothes to trade, or better still a little gold, could exchange them for rice with "old people" or with Khmer Rouge cadres who had accumulated extra rations by failing to report deaths from disease and malnutrition.

For many, only these illegal transactions kept them alive. Thousands of others died — from physical exhaustion, poor and inadequate food, lack of sanitation, illness and disease or were executed. Malaria was rife. Medicines were unprocurable and medical care minimal or non-existent. Many starved and many more were killed for quite absurd crimes such as begging for rations to be increased, or for complaints overheard by spies about the harshness of the regime. To ask for more food was to be ungrateful to Angkar for what one had been given: it was to criticize the beneficence of Angkar. The cadres always assured people that their sufferings were as nothing compared to those the cadres themselves had put up with during the civil war. Armed Khmer Rouge troops kept people in the new villages in a state of terror. Arrests were made at night, for reasons no-one knew. Victims were marched off into the forest where they were shot or more usually clubbed to death with an axe or hoe. Sometimes the bodies were buried in shallow graves, or left to lie where they fell to be discovered later by work details cutting bamboo or families foraging for food. In the new villages the only punishment for any misdemeanour was death.

In some new villages children over the age of about eight were taken from their families to work in children's labour brigades under the watchful eye of Khmer Rouge guards. Older youths and girls made up their own brigades. Many children died of disease, abuse and malnutrition. Parents would simply be informed in due course that their child was dead. If they wept, or showed any signs of grief, they were brutally reprimanded for indulging in bourgeois and individualistic sentimentality. Their children had died for the revolution: they should be proud, not sorrowful, and determine to strive even harder themselves to the same end. A similar attitude was taken towards a wife showing sorrow over the execution of her husband, or children for their father. Anyone executed was an enemy; regret for such a person indicated failure either to love the revolution or to recognize the justice of Angkar. For as the Khmer Rouge cadres repeatedly stated: "Nothing to gain by keeping them alive; nothing to lose by doing away with them." Even the killing of someone without reason could be justified, for it was "better to kill an innocent person than to leave an enemy alive".

In September and October 1975, a second series of new villages was set up in remote parts of the country for "new people" swept up in a second great movement of population. Most families involved were evacuees from Phnom Penh who had settled in the Southwest Zone provinces of Kandal, Takeo, and Kampot. They were usually transported by train or truck mainly to the Northern and Northwestern Zone provinces of Oddar Mean Chey, Siem Reap, Battambang, or Pursat. In some cases "new people" were inveigled into volunteering for relocation by the promise that they could go to their home villages; or they were told they would be returning to Phnom Penh. Others were simply ordered to collect their belongings and be ready to depart on a specified date. Many left in hope, only to see those hopes dashed under the concentration-camp conditions of the new villages. And progressively all hope died — for an improvement with the return of Sihanouk, for an armed uprising against the Khmer Rouge, even for a change of heart on the part of the regime. Men like Pin Yathay watched their children, their elderly parents and their close relatives die, as they struggled to keep the remaining members of their families alive.

The death toll in the new villages was appalling. One group of 500 families (some 2,500 people) was transported from Takeo province in January 1976 to one of a string of villages along the foothills of the Cardamon range in Pursat province. For fifteen months the people in these new villages struggled to grow and gather enough food to survive. At the end of that time half were dead. So terrible were the conditions that in April 1977, 8,000 were moved to villages a few kilometres from Pursat town. Even there, however, disease, malnutrition and the savagery of Khmer Rouge punishment continued to take their toll. At the end of 1978, of those originally transported together from Takeo province only 500, or 20 per cent, remained.[3]

Some had tried to escape, but escape was a crime punishable immediately by death. Anyone travelling outside the village where he or she lived had to carry the written permission of the chief Khmer Rouge cadre. Even with a pass anyone moving in a border area was suspect, and could expect to be arrested and questioned about his or her movements. The only alternative was to take to the jungle. But there other dangers lurked. Apart from lack of food and water, wild animals and poisonous snakes and insects, and the possibility of getting lost, there was the additional danger of booby traps and land mines on many paths approaching the border, and the constant threat of coming across a Khmer Rouge patrol. Anyone caught was either killed on the spot, the body left in the jungle for others to stumble across, or returned to the village from which they had fled to be publicly executed as a warning to others.

But despite all warnings, many did try to escape — and many managed to reach Thailand or Vietnam. The choice was one between a slow death from disease and starvation, or a quick death at the hands of the Khmer Rouge if caught escaping. Only family responsibilities and the sheer distances to cover prevented more making the attempt. For those in provinces far from the Thai border escape to the West was practically an impossibility. But those "new people" transported during the second deportation in late 1975 suddenly found themselves much closer to the border. Those living in villages in the Oddar Mean Chey or Pursat areas could hope to escape via the jungles of the Dangrek or Cardamon Ranges. The going was dangerous and rough, but the chance of being stopped by a patrol was correspondingly less.

Many who escaped during 1975 and 1976 did so because they had no reason to stay: the regime was too harsh, especially towards "new people" in new villages in the North and Northwest Zones; it gave them nothing in return for the loyalty and dedication it demanded to its revolutionary goals. The pitiless brutality and inflexibility of the youthful Khmer Rouge cadres, their unjustified and unaccountable power over life and death and their heartless unconcern for human suffering and sorrow all contributed to destroy whatever commitment those on the losing side had been prepared to make once the Revolution had triumphed. In the new villages of the new Kampuchea countless thousands died, 70 or 80 per cent of all those transported in some places. But the full count of those who suffered such brutal and unnecessary deaths will never be known.

CHAPTER 6

Communes and Mobile Brigades

On 6 September 1976, the people of Maesor Prachan were called together for a mass political meeting where they were told it was time to take a further step in implementing the revolution. Individual rights, it was said, were a carry-over from the former regime. Everyone should learn to think only in terms of the communal interest. In order to further this change from individual to communal consciousness, Angkar had decreed that communal dining should be introduced immediately. No advance warning was given and communal dining, which had been introduced earlier in most other regions, began next day. The title of hamlet chief (me-phum) was officially changed to head of the cooperative (me-sahakor). The seven hamlet cooperatives together constituted the commune of Maesor Prachan.

These changes were accompanied by a purge of village officials. Yon, the hamlet chief of Phum Andong, lost his positions and was replaced by the deputy hamlet chief in Phum Loeu, a large, fat, flabby man called Prak (literally meaning "silver"), who was vicious in his hatred of anyone from Phnom Penh. "When he looked at us "new people", Bun recounted, "you could see the hatred in his eyes. When he had dealings with the "old people", he spoke nicely and smiled. But immediately he turned his face to address us he became angry." Prak came from a very poor family and was brutal in his implementation of Khmer

Rouge policies. He "ruled" Phum Andong as a tyrant exercising absolute power.

The change to communal eating signified a hardening of Khmer Rouge policies on social transformation and represented a new step forward in the communalization of Kampuchean society. People were called upon to renounce their individual rights by turning over all their remaining private belongings to the village authorities, including all cooking and eating utensils, and anything whose possession might hinder the full development of communal consciousness. To make sure that everyone complied Khmer Rouge militia and village spies searched all houses the week communal dining began. "New people", of course were primary targets. Food, such as ripening bananas, was taken before it could be eaten. Every knife or spoon, every dish or bowl or pot was confiscated. So too were any books or photographs, paper, pencils, or pens. Private study, or reading, was considered anti-social and non-productive. The Khmer Rouge ripped the pages out of some books to use as cigarette paper; others were burned. They seized any radios or watches or jewellery they found and took every bicycle in the village, stacking them in the village pagoda for official use only. There were over a hundred bicycles and the Khmer Rouge cadres rode them until they were punctured or broken; then exchanged them for others. None was ever repaired. After the searches, people commented bitterly that they were prepared to give everything to Angkar — except their wives.

Bun had managed to smuggle a few books past the Khmer Rouge checkpoints during the evacuation from Phnom Penh. These included a couple of school text books in Khmer, and one art book in English on Angkor, the great ruined former capital of the Khmer Empire, abandoned in the fourteenth century. These he had carefully wrapped in plastic, together with some good clothes, and buried in the garden. Luckily the Khmer Rouge did not find them, though only very occasionally after that could he risk digging them up to read. Nor did they find his fish net which he did not surrender for communal use. It was too dangerous to fish himself, even at night; but there was always the possibility that he might have need of it later. The Khmer Rouge did find Bun's drawing compass: it turned up later in the village hospital, its sharp point used by the "dentist" to probe the teeth of his patients!

What Bun missed most during this time was not being able to draw. For almost four years he never held a pencil in his hand. He possessed neither crayons nor paper, and there was no way

A former Government officer is arrested.

Communal dining is introduced.

to obtain either. Besides, to draw cartoons would have been dangerous, and would in all probability have led to prison, interrogation, and even torture and death. But the images were printed on his mind, and he swore to himself that one day he would draw a record of all that he had seen.

The move to communal dining was very unpopular. Even "old people" who until then had entirely supported the Khmer Rouge were unhappy at the change. But no-one dared openly to complain. Many people tried to keep some private belongings, but the Khmer Rouge maintained that everything belonged to Angkar and to the society as a whole. Few people were convinced, but the searches were thorough because the Khmer Rouge knew this. Houses were ransacked while their occupants were working in the fields and when they returned home, exhausted, there was nothing they could do.

So abrupt was the transition to communal dining that no prior preparations had been made. People had to squat on the ground to eat. Only later were large communal dining halls built in each hamlet. There, people ate in groups of eight to a table around a single pot of soup. A bell was rung at meal times — the first time for children and the elderly, the second for able-bodied adults. The food usually consisted of rice soup, fish, and water plants. Besides *tracuon*, the stem of a water lily called *pralit* was commonly eaten, often in the form of a sour soup with tamarind. After each meal, everybody had to take their eating utensils to the kitchen where they were washed and placed ready for the next meal. Food was poor in quality, very monotonous, and there was seldom enough of it. A popular saying had it that: "We eat everything with four legs, except chairs and tables". It was strictly forbidden, however, for anyone to search for or eat food privately or in the family. Though each family was still responsible for growing fruit and vegetables in home gardens, and for raising chickens or ducks, none had the right to eat their produce. Vegetables were gathered or poultry requisitioned only by order of the hamlet authorities for communal needs. This did not mean that fruit was not stolen whenever possible, but great care had to be taken. Someone had to stand watch. "Old people" as well as "new" sometimes managed to hide some food to be eaten secretly at night, after everyone was asleep. Some even managed to kill and cook a chicken. It had to be done at night, steamed in a kettle whose spout could be blocked to prevent any smell escaping, and eaten under a blanket (even at the height of summer).

Opposition to communal dining was particularly strong among the small Cham minority who lived in the village. The

Communal dining first established outdoors.

September 1976 — all private possessions are confiscated.

Cham had settled in Kampuchea after their state of Champa on the coast of what is now central Vietnam was destroyed by the Vietnamese in the fifteenth century. Most were fisherfolk, living peacefully side by side with their Kampuchean neighbours. They were despised by the Khmer Rouge, however, both for having allegedly abandoned their country to the hated Vietnamese (something the Khmer Rouge proclaimed themselves determined never to do), and for being a culturally distinct minority with their own language, religion (Islam), and customs. Khmer Rouge policy was to break up Cham villages, and force their assimilation by forbidding use of the Cham language or practice of their religion. This had been done in Maesor Prachan when the Chams living in the hamlet of Krahamkor next door to Phum Andong had been dispersed throughout the other hamlets.

The Cham had converted to Islam after settling in Kampuchea and this set them apart from the Buddhist Khmer. They kept to themselves in tight-knit communities, exchanging fish for rice with their Khmer neighbours, and religiously avoiding the eating of pork. When communal dining was introduced they were forced to eat the same as everyone else, including rice gruel sometimes containing a few morsels of pork fat. Two old men in Maesor Prachan refused to eat with the rest of the hamlet. After a week of boycotting communal dining the two were arrested and shot for refusing to obey the orders of Angkar, and as a warning to others. Later a Cham youth caught cooking a chicken in his home was arrested and sent to the gaol of Snaypol. Like others sent for re-education he was never seen again. Repression of the Cham steadily increased during the next two years, as it did for other ethnic minorities, both indigenous (the various tribal minorities) and non-indigenous (the Chinese).

To act as the "front line troops" in the accelerated struggle to transform Kampuchean society, new communal labour forces were constituted. These were known as mobile groups, or brigades (Krom chalat), and were composed of all young unmarried men and women between the ages of sixteen and thirty. Mobile brigades were to act as "shock troops" in the national drive for increased productivity, and could be assigned to work sites anywhere in the district. They were organized along military lines modelled on the Khmer Rouge armed forces. Twelve workers made up an "A" group, or section, three of which constituted a "B" group (platoon) while three "B" groups made up a "C" group (i.e. a company of 108 people). Each "C" group usually slept, ate and worked together. Three of Bun's cousins were in his "C" group, but none in his "A" group.

The mobile brigade builds new living quarters.

A new phase of revolutionary development is announced.

One of the first tasks of the Maesor Prachan mobile brigade was to bring in the harvest at the Tuol Don Teov work site. Then in January 1977 work began on a new irrigation canal in Peareang district to link up newly constructed 100-metre square paddies with the Tonle Toch river. This was such a major project that other mobile brigades were also assigned to work on sections of the canal. The first work site was situated ten kilometres from Maesor Prachan. The brigade loaded building materials onto ox carts and began constructing long huts to sleep a hundred people and communal dining halls and kitchens. Until these were completed everyone ate and slept on the ground.

The formation of these mobile brigades marked a new phase in the increasing militarization of economic production. Not only was discipline at work sites of a military rigour, but each work project was described in military terms, as a military operation mounted on military lines. At the compulsory public meetings called in the village to inform everyone of this new phase in the revolutionary development of the country, it was explained that such new large-scale irrigation projects constituted the "front line" of the battle to build the new Kampuchea. Those who carried on the struggle at the construction front would be supported by the "rear", the villages where women, children and the elderly would also have to work harder to make up for the absence of younger, stronger workers.

Everything was done in launching the mobile brigades to generate a spirit of active cooperation and revolutionary fervour. The work site was the battle ground where the construction army would "struggle", in a militant sense (prayot), with great courage to build dykes and dig the new canal. And this project was part of a general offensive; workers on the site were "fighters"; they were at war in order to achieve a new "victory" in constructing the country. In achieving this victory, brigade members were told, they were serving Angkar, the people, and the revolution. This economic offensive was part of the overall programme of independence and self-sufficiency , coupled with new border attacks on Vietnam, which would restore Kampuchea to prosperity and greatness, and retain the nation's independence and territorial integrity.

Every agricultural worker became a soldier in the war to build, and by building defend, the country. Labourers sallying forth to repair an irrigation dyke were "launching an offensive": a summer rice crop successfully harvested in the face of rising floods was a "victory over nature". Sometimes this military phraseology was taken to ludicrous extremes. Those who climbed the sugar palms to tap the juice which was boiled down to give palm sugar were known as "pilots" in the "air army" of sugar makers!

When mobile groups were rotated at the work site, vast meetings were organized of all the new groups taking part in the project to inform all worker-soldiers of what Angkar expected of them. Thousands of youths and girls from all over the district squatted in the dry rice paddies while speaker after speaker reiterated the familiar themes of service, participation and solidarity in the glorious revolutionary struggle to construct the new Kampuchea. Victory depended on unity: it was the responsibility of every worker to ensure the success of such a great project. Thus would Kampuchea achieve true independence and sovereignty, and happiness for all in working together — no longer dispossessed and exploited as under the traitorous Lon Nol regime, but true masters of their own destiny. By taking part in this glorious national task, worker-soldiers were simultaneously transmuting themselves into new socialist men and women, single-mindedly devoted to Angkar and the state. After the political speeches came displays by revolutionary dancers and songs of struggle and victory. Attendance was compulsory, except for the sick. Men and women sat separately, and listened quietly. No-one spoke out, no-one demonstrated their revolutionary enthusiasm until told to do so.

Work hours in the mobile brigades were increased over those for village work groups. Work began at 4 a.m. and continued to noon when lunch was served. The afternoon session began at 1 p.m. and lasted until 6. After the evening meal everyone usually slept, exhausted, to rise again at 3.45 the next morning. Work was entirely by hand: no machines of any kind were used on brigade work sites. The Khmer Rouge cadres told brigade members that the Khmer people were so brave and strong that they did not need machines. After all, they had defeated the American imperialists with their bare hands. By not becoming reliant on machines they would preserve their national independence. Men dug with hoes, or loaded dirt into baskets with their hands. Women carried the baskets on their heads to dump the dirt onto the dykes on either side of the canal. Everyone had to work hard, for fear of criticism by Khmer Rouge cadres, who would sit watching, listening to revolutionary songs broadcast from Phnom Penh on their transistor radios. Poor work or laziness meant that the regular section meetings called for criticism and self-criticism would be prolonged. In that case everyone in the section suffered, and missed their sleep!

Sections were always composed of a mixture of "old" and "new people". Chiefs and deputy chiefs were appointed for each section, and changed frequently. Some were good, Bun thought, and some were harsh and vindictive. Mobile brigades from different villages often competed when working on a large site involving five or even ten thousand workers. Brigades vied with each other to see which could construct the longest section of dyke, or dig the best canal. Some brigades even began work an hour early in order to prove their revolutionary dedication and increase their productivity. Bun's brigade never began work before 4 a.m., and yet still ranked among the best and most productive in the region. Great care had to be taken not to dig so hard that a hoe or shovel handle broke. Whoever was responsible would be severely criticised as an enemy of the state, and would be a marked man. It was even more serious if a plough were broken, for the culprit might even be arrested and sent for re-education.

Conversation was not forbidden on the work site, provided it did not lead to any slackening of effort. But Bun made a decision not to speak at all if he could help it — mainly to avoid saying anything which could in any way be interpreted as critical of the regime. It was a decision he wisely kept to — especially after an incident in which one of Bun's cousins was arrested after complaining that the work was not good for him, and he was weary of it. He had been a student in Phnom Penh, but was accused of being an agent of the CIA, trying to undermine the commitment of other workers. He was sent to the district prison in Peareang and was not seen again.

Men and women were strictly segregated at all times in the mobile brigades. They slept in different huts and ate separately. Banter or even conversation between them was discouraged, and soon came to be completely forbidden. As time went on, work became progressively harder and rules increasingly strictly applied. Both men and women ate in their own sections. Food was prepared by special details of cooks who were always "old people". The job of cook was much sought after, both because it was much less onerous than working out in the sun, and because one could eat much better. The Khmer Rouge did not trust "new people" to be cooks.

The cooks usually prepared special meals for the higher Khmer Rouge officials, in return for which they were permitted extra privileges, such as freedom to leave the work site in order to obtain supplies, and to use bicycles which otherwise none but Khmer Rouge cadres could ride. The food they cooked for the

Even eye-contact between brother and sister is forbidden.

Collecting dung out of work hours.

brigade workers was of consistently low quality; the same dishes every meal — rice soup with vegetables and occasionally a few pieces of fish or chicken in it. Hygiene was poor, and flies gathered in swarms. While eating, Bun had constantly to wave one hand to keep flies from settling on his lips. Sick people ate separately, but instead of being given special food in order to renew their strength, they received less to eat in accordance with the constantly repeated dictum: those who do not work do not eat. There was an incentive, therefore, for those who were sick to try to keep working so as to obtain normal rations. But those at the end of their physical limits were more susceptible to disease, and many who fell sick did not recover.

Initially work on the special project sites continued for two weeks at a time on a rotational basis. Brigades which had been relieved by others returned to their villages for two weeks to a month to help plough and prepare the paddies, grow vegetables and perform their usual tasks, before going back to the work site again. Later they spent longer periods on the work sites as was usually the case in other Zones. Sometimes they were away from the village for three months at a time. Once one project was finished, the brigade was assigned another. At harvest time they moved from village to village more rapidly, to help wherever they were most needed.

During 1977, the men's group and women's group were usually assigned to different sites. When they were working on the same site, segregation was even stricter than before. A brother could no longer speak to his own sister without first obtaining permission from the group leader. Even then the conversation could only take place in the presence of the group leader himself. Not so much as a smile could be exchanged. Any infringement of these rules met with punishment — for the first instance in the form of severe criticism at a group session, after which the culprit would have to demonstrate his contrition by working especially hard at any difficult and unpleasant jobs to which he was directed by his group leader. A subsequent offence could lead to arrest.

The extreme lengths to which this puritan division of the sexes was taken in Democratic Kampuchea can be illustrated by an incident in which Bun was involved in December 1977. His mobile group was assigned to work in Phum Maesor Prachan hamlet where his favourite aunt lived. Bun was very fond of her and had not seen her for a long time. When he met her suddenly one day he impulsively took her hand. "I forgot, you see", Bun later explained. "I missed her, and I was pleased to see her." Immediately a Khmer Rouge cadre shouted at him. Bun dropped his aunt's hand and jumped away, but the crime had been committed. A meeting of Bun's "A" group was immediately called to deal with this serious breach of the rules. Bun was severely criticised for his failure to develop a revolutionary morality. His action proved that he had failed to change his mode of thinking and failed to renounce the corrupt morality of the old regime. It was a most serious charge. Bun apologized. His group leader advised him to change his ways, or he would be punished most severely. Bun had no need to ask what that punishment would be: he would be sent for re-education.

It is difficult to understand the Khmer Rouge attitude towards sexual morality. At one level it had to do with forging a purity of will and dedication to the new Kampuchea. Only Angkar should be the recipient of unquestioning devotion and loyalty. Anything which detracted from a pure and total commitment to Angkar as embodiment of the national good had to be opposed. Close family relationships could form the basis for conspiracy against the regime. In any contest between duty and dedication to Angkar and any claim on the individual by family or friends, Angkar had to come first. The focus of any alternative commitment had to be undermined — and that meant, above all, weakening traditionally strong family ties. Both communal eating and the refusal to permit any exceptions even within the family to the rules on sexual morality had this desired effect. So too did the education to which children were subjected: the aim was to weaken the family as a cohesive unit, so that where a conflict of interests between family and Angkar arose, Angkar could claim, and receive, the first loyalty of every Kampuchean.

The effect of prohibitions on the display of any public emotion directed towards family members (and Kampucheans have never been overly demonstrative people) was not only to destroy all natural contacts, but also to introduce tensions into even the closest family relationships. A grown son could not so much as touch his mother's hand in public. Husbands and wives, especially "new people", could not walk side by side. They were afraid to show affection, even in private. Spies were everywhere, and the walls of houses were made only of woven palm. Later, when Bun married, he seldom took his wife's hand, even in his own home, in case it should be reported to the village authorities and taken as indicating a refusal on the part of both of them to put behind them the old morality and dedicate themselves to the revolution alone.

During 1977 more village cadres were purged, to be replaced by men chosen for their dedication and ruthlessness in implementing the new and harsher policies. Without exception these changes brought to positions of power and authority cadres from the poorest backgrounds, men who could be depended on to act without pity towards those who had been their social superiors. Eak, the village chief of Maesor Prachan, was ousted in mid-1977 to be replaced by his deputy Lim, a dark skinned, strongly-built man who had previously made a living as a cattle smuggler, selling stolen animals across the border into southern Vietnam. The village committee was reduced to two men, Lim and his deputy, Suon, previously the committee member in charge of the economy. Under these two, food supplied to the dining hall and mobile brigades was progressively reduced, as higher quotas were creamed off by Angkar. Ironically, while Lim and Suon both lost their lives in later purges which followed the downfall of So Phim, Eak, and others purged earlier, survived.

Not only were rules more vigorously enforced in 1977, but hours of labour for the mobile groups were again extended. A third session of work was introduced after the evening meal. This usually lasted from 7 to 10 p.m., and meant that sleep was reduced to less than six hours a night. Work at night was either by moonlight, or under the light of palm-leaf flares. The strain of working and living under such conditions, now seven days a week, week in and week out, was debilitating. Work was regulated by the blowing of whistles at the work site. The only allowed break was to take a drink of water or go to the toilet. Makeshift toilets were constructed near the work site to reduce time lost. Fear of punishment was ever present. Although the Khmer Rouge cadres themselves could be avoided, no-one was ever sure that someone else would not report something overheard. Some workers tried to ingratiate themselves with group leaders by reporting on their fellow workers.

Every evening each "A" group met for criticism and self-criticism. Meetings of the whole brigade took place every three days. Sessions usually opened with an harangue by the group leader on the need always to respect Angkar, and to work for Angkar to the utmost of one's capacity. Chief of Bun's "A" group was a short, weedy youth of seventeen named Eang. He was from a poor peasant family, and clearly enjoyed his position of power. Eang was brutal and crude in his manner towards the group, and delighted in keeping everyone working continuously. He was critical of his charges, accusing then of laziness and a lack of dedication to Angkar. These were serious crimes, and group members vied with each other to exculpate themselves through self-criticism. Bun frequently admitted to being a little bit lazy, to having felt able to work harder, to having talked too much (even though it was his policy not to talk at all). Even if he had worked as hard as he could, he would never say so. No work was ever perfect: it was always possible to do better. And how could they match the bounty of Angkar? Angkar provided everything for them. How could they ever repay such a debt?

During 1977 the long hours of hard work began to take their toll. Sickness became more common. Many people contracted mosquito-borne diseases or intestinal disorders. Malaria was particularly prevalent. Bun's family had three mosquito nets for seven people which they had brought with them from Phnom Penh. If one contracted malaria there was nothing for it but to let the fever take its course, as the local traditional remedy was ineffectual.

On two occasions during 1977 Bun was so sick that he had to be sent to hospital. The first was for two weeks, but the second was for three months after he contracted dysentery as a result of poor working conditions, long hours of labour, and poor food unhygienically prepared. On the second occasion, his family feared for his life, but he slowly recovered. Both times he was admitted to the village hospital in what was formerly the primary school in Phum Maesor Prachan. On the second occasion he had to be carried on a stretcher, known popularly as going by "bamboo ambulance". Patients had to bring their own blankets, eating utensils from the communal dining hall, and anything else they might need.

The village hospital was staffed by Khmer Rouge "people's doctors", cadres trained for six months in simple health care and the prescription of medicines. Nurses, teenage boys and girls, were given three months' training in the district or regional hospital. Both doctors and nurses were centrally appointed. "New people" were never accepted since it was feared that they would "poison" the patients — especially any "old people" or cadres. In the regional hospital operations were used as training sessions for student medical cadres. The operating theatre was a large mosquito net draped around a bed. Other patients could also watch what was happening. The Khmer Rouge compared this favourably with the old regime: then doctors operated in secret; now everyone could see what they were doing.

The chief doctor in Maesor Prachan hospital made his rounds early each morning. It was his duty to examine every patient and prescribe the medicines to be taken that day. These

A sick worker being forced to re-join his mobile brigade.

A mobile brigade constructs an irrigation canal.

were then dispensed by the nurses. In addition to various kinds of pills, two types of injections were given — a red fluid which the doctor called "Vitamin B12" and a colourless fluid called "Vitamin C". They were stored in old Pepsi Cola or Coke bottles. Injections were much feared by the patients as they often resulted in abscesses from the use of unhygienic needles. The same syringe needle was used for all patients, and Bun estimated that while he was in hospital, fully 70 percent of all patients given injections contracted an infection. Coconut milk was used as serum for serious cases and, not surprisingly, most did not recover. The only other form of treatment was acupuncture, performed by one of the doctors using needles made from steel guitar strings. This also often resulted in infection.

Bun counted himself particularly fortunate not to have developed abscesses during his long illness, especially while he was receiving injections. He was appalled by the lack of hygiene and the primitive conditions. Doctors and nurses both had what seemed a callous disregard for their patients. They appeared to care little for human life, or suffering. Cures were seen as experiments: if they worked that was interesting; if they didn't, that was too bad. It was all put down to experience. Something else could be tried next time. Conditions of care made recovery difficult. Patients were bombarded day and night with loud music, revolutionary songs and political speeches. They found it difficult to sleep, but could not ask for the loudspeakers to be turned down as this would be taken as selfish, individualistic, and anti-revolutionary.

Once a week all patients were assembled for political instruction. At all times patients knew they were being spied upon by the nurses. The Khmer Rouge were determined not to permit any malingering. Patients who were well enough ate in the hospital dining hall. Anyone whose appetite began to return was believed to have recovered. The medical cadres applied the universal rule: "Those who eat can work". Even patients still recovering their strength were given work to do, helping around the hospital, husking rice, or loosening soil in the hospital vegetable garden. The moment patients were considered to be eating too much, they were discharged. Any patient who died was buried in the hospital grounds, and the family informed. Relatives were not permitted to take the corpse away for burial elsewhere, or to perform any Buddhist funeral ceremonies.

Bun attributed his eventual recovery more to the care he received from his aunt than to the prescriptions of the doctors. As his mother lived in another hamlet, she could only rarely obtain permission to visit him. But his aunt lived in Phum Maesor Prachan, and could come to care for him without first going to the surly hamlet authorities. She used to bring Bun tea secretly brewed from marijuana leaves which was sweet to the taste and made him sleepy, but was good for diarrhoea. The only hospital medicine he liked was one made from honey: it provided energy to supplement the poor diet. Once he had recovered somewhat, Bun enjoyed his stay in hospital, despite the boredom of having nothing to read and only the loudspeaker to listen to. The work he was given was light compared to working in the fields, and he tried not to eat too much so as to prolong his period of recovery. Eventually, however, he was declared fit, and sent back to the mobile brigade.

Each morning brigade workers were woken by the sound of a bell. Once out of bed, they had to line up in their various groups for inspection by group leaders. Even those who were sick had to attend, for it was at the inspection that group leaders decided who was well enough to work in the fields and who sick enough to be let off. Anyone suspected of malingering would be sent to work. Those considered sick were examined by the doctors attached to the mobile brigade. They were given medication and allowed to rest, but their food ration was cut.

During times of planting and harvest, when the mobile brigades returned to work in their home villages, members did not live in their own homes. Instead they were billetted with those "old people" who had large houses. Brigade members ate at different times from the rest of the people. Thus even in their own hamlets youths in the mobile brigade continued to live and work as a separate labour force, having minimal contact with the rest of the village.

As the time of planting approached the mobile brigades prepared the land, repaired irrigation channels, and controlled vermin. A hundred women would be assigned to cross and recross the large square paddy fields to catch small freshwater crabs which would otherwise destroy the young rice. Men dug for mice and large rice rats whose holes perforated the paddy dykes. Once the land was prepared, planting began. The men carried heavy bundles of rice seedlings often several kilometres to the work site where they were planted out. Thirty-six men or women — one "B" group — were expected to plant one hectare of paddy in the morning and sometimes planting continued until late at night. Working in the evening and at night, however, was a relief after working through the heat of the day, for April and May are the hottest months in Kampuchea. Sometimes, however,

At Maesor Prachan hospital.

Planting rice in the paddies.

after working late to complete a task, a brigade would receive orders assigning them to a new project elsewhere. These had to be obeyed immediately, whatever the time. Members would have to pack their clothes and bedding, and march perhaps ten kilometres to be ready to start work again at 5 a.m.

There was no escape for brigade members from the ceaseless round of work. Even the few moments they had to themselves were taken up weaving palm hats, mending clothes, massaging each other, tending cuts or bruises, or attending section criticism sessions. Little wonder that brigade members sought escape through sickness. The only concession accorded the women was the three days each month they were allowed off heavy work during menstruation. Every woman took advantage of the break, even though many were no longer menstruating at all. At such time women from "old" families were usually assigned as cooks' assistants working in the kitchen, while women from "new" families had to mix dung and dirt to form the manure used on the rice fields.

Everyone worked longer hours at harvest time, even the children. The school was closed, and children were sent into the paddies to help gather up bundles of rice, and to glean every last grain that had fallen during harvesting. Everyone helped to bring in the crop, but the hardest work was performed by the mobile groups. In the village old men led buffaloes and oxen to thresh the grain by trampling it under foot, while women swept the rice into piles.

After lunch came what was known as the "socialist hour" when everyone had to work together to prepare natural fertilizer for the next rice crop. Women and children collected cattle dung while the men cut green plants. Plants and dung were then mixed in layers in pits to make compost. Harvesting continued during the afternoon work session, and after the evening meal everyone gathered again at the threshing area. There bundles of paddy were threshed by hand or under foot, while children gathered up the scattered grain. Work continued by moonlight or kerosene lanterns, the property of the commune. During threshing, grains of rice sometimes flew into people's eyes.

But an even worse place to work was in the husking hall, under the pagoda in Phum Andong. According to Bun, the close and cramped conditions made it a hellish place where sweating villagers crowded closely together. Husking was carried out in this confined space so as not to lose either rice or bran. It was unbearably hot, even in the evenings, and the atmosphere was full of dust, rice chaff, and the stench of perspiration. Men and women used primitive grinders to husk the paddy rice, and hand-turned fans to separate the grain from the husk. Stamp hammers were used to bruise off the outer skin and produce white rice. Groups competed with each other to husk the required daily target of 200 kilograms of white rice per group. Any group working slowly was criticized by the others, and by village cadres.

The harvest would be completed hamlet by hamlet. That from Phum Andong was always brought in first. The people of Phum Andong had the reputation of being the hardest workers in Maesor Prachan. After the rice was threshed and husked, army trucks arrived to take much of it away. Khmer Rouge officials said the rice was needed "to support the Revolution". Village cadres explained to the people that whereas under the former regime the poor were taxed heavily so that the rich could live in luxury in Phnom Penh, under the new regime rice taken away by the government was given gladly for the benefit of Angkar and to further the Revolution. When the rice left in the village proved insufficient to last until the next harvest (as happened in 1977 despite greatly increased production), cadres told the villagers it was their own fault. Any shortage was not because new government procurement taxes were too high, but because people had not been working hard enough. If they wanted more food they should work harder. However, when a few items such as black cloth, tobacco, a little kerosene, or occasionally a tiny piece of soap were distributed by the village authorities, much was made of the bounty and compassion of Angkar.

On 5 October 1977, Bun married Phiny Kang, a girl five years younger than himself, in a mass ceremony in Maesor Prachan. Phiny came from a "new family". Her father Bophaphann Kang, had been the chief of Chhlong district in Kratie province under the former regime but had fled to Phnom Penh during the war. The family had come to Maesor Prachan since Kang was a close friend of one of Bun's uncles, who had often told him of his home village in the rich rice land of Peareang district. In December 1975 Kang had been denounced and arrested by the Khmer Rouge, together with his oldest son, a former lieutenant in the Lon Nol army. Both had been sent to Pearang gaol for re-education, after which they were executed. Before Bun and Phiny left Maesor Prachan in February 1979, Phiny was to lose two more brothers and two sisters out of her ten remaining siblings.

Marriages took place only twice a year in Maesor Prachan. On this occasion sixty couples were married — "old people" in

Threshing and husking the rice.

the morning, and "new people" in the afternoon. It was most unusual for boys and girls from "old" and "new" families to marry, as the Khmer Rouge did not approve of such mixed marriages; permission had been given only once in Maesor Prachan. Boys had to be at least twenty and girls eighteen before they could get married. Both were usually keen to marry, for then they could remain in the village and escape the long absences from their families spent working in the mobile groups. When the village authorities announced the date for a communal wedding ceremony, men not already "engaged" began approaching girls in the same hamlet. If turned down by one, they often tried another, and negotiations between families sometimes continued to the last minute. Once married, the couple lived together, though young married men could still be drafted for special duties such as timber cutting which took them away for weeks at a time.

Bun did not have any wish to get married after he arrived in Maesor Prachan. He had intended to wait until he had completed his degree and found a good job, but in Democratic Kampuchea this was an impossible dream. Living as he did provided no basis for the future. Bun had got to know Phiny over a period of two years because she lived in the same hamlet and was a friend of his sister. She could visit the Ung family, or Bun and his sister could visit the Kangs, without first requesting permission from the village authorities. Phiny was in the women's mobile group, and sometimes worked on the same site as Bun, though of course the two could never exchange a word, or even so much as smile at each other, without risking criticism.

In Maesor Prachan there was little official pressure to get married in 1975 or 1976. In other regions marriages were frequently arranged by the authorities and were compulsory. A friend of Bun's whom he met in Phnom Penh after the Pol Pot regime had been overthrown, had been forced to marry a girl he had never seen before, one found for him by the village authorities. But in Maesor Prachan marriages were still personally arranged. The family of the bridegroom had to ask the bride's family for their daughter in marriage and, if the bride's family agreed, the hamlet chief was informed. Permission was routinely given except between couples from "old" and "new" families. Marriages usually took place between couples in the same hamlet, though permission could be granted for marriages between couples in different hamlets within the same village. No possibility existed for a man to marry a girl from another village.

By 1977 Bun had changed his mind about getting married. He was then twenty-five. One reason for his change of heart was that he sensed some antagonism towards him on the part of the Khmer Rouge cadres. He had already crossed swords with Prak, the hamlet chief, when he was recovering towards the end of his three month stay in hospital. One of the doctors told a cadre Bun was eating well and was better. Soon after, Prak came to the hospital and accused Bun of malingering. Bun had protested that he was still regaining his strength, but he knew the hamlet chief suspected his commitment to the new Kampuchea. If Bun did not marry, the Khmer Rouge might think it was because he did not want any family ties — and that might mean that he intended to rebel against the regime. At least this was what the Ung family believed, and Bun's mother wanted him to marry. Too many young men had already been arrested on no more substantial grounds than the suspicion or hostility of the cadres.

Bun agreed to get married the next time a communal ceremony was announced, and informed the village authorities of his decision. The date of the ceremony was not announced until the evening before it was to take place. At the time Bun was working with his mobile brigade. The next morning he was given a new set of black pyjamas as a parting present by the brigade leader, and sent on his way. The day of the mass ceremony was a holiday only for those taking part. Each family was allowed to have one member present as witness: everyone else worked as usual. Bun's and Phiny's mothers both attended.

The ceremony took place in two parts in the pagoda at Phum Kampong Trea, one of the other hamlets making up Maesor Prachan. "New people" were married in the afternoon after a communal lunch eaten in the pagoda grounds. The pagoda served as a community hall, for political meetings and other official ceremonies. All the Buddha images had been removed, and the paintings on the walls defaced. Everyone wore their usual black pyjamas, Ho Chi Minh sandals and neck scarf. One of the village officials, a man named Soun, opened proceedings with a political speech about socialism in the new Kampuchea. He reminded the assembled couples that they had to prove their dedication to Angkar after marriage by continuing to work for the Revolution. Both husband and wife should be selfless, and never forget their duty to the community and to the state. Together the sixty couples pledged themselves to Angkar, and promised to perform any duty demanded of them. They were then declared man and wife: no monks chanted prayers; no traditional rituals were per-

The community creche.

The production of "number one manure."

formed. After the brief ceremony everyone returned to their hamlets.

After his marriage, Bun went to live with his wife's family. The day after the ceremony both newlyweds were back at work — only "old people" had a further two days' holiday. It was usual after a couple were married for both to be sent on separate work details for two or three weeks some distance from the village, to prevent them being together. This was to underline the reality of their marriage vows to Angkar. Not only had a young couple to leave each other without complaint, but they had to set off cheerfully, full of joy at this new opportunity to work for the Revolution. Four days after his wedding Bun was sent to repair irrigation dykes at Phum Yot hamlet for a fortnight. Two days after his return Phiny was assigned to join a fishing expedition to a place forty kilometres from the village. For a month she cut and salted fish for smoking. Only after she returned were the couple permitted to spend some time together.

Bun had hoped that working in the village would be easier than in a mobile brigade. But those who remained in the village, married men and women, children and the elderly, worked harder than ever towards the end of 1977. Early each morning children below the age of six were left at the community child-minding centre, an area underneath two adjoining houses where oxen and buffaloes were kept at night. Each morning the area had to be cleaned before use, but even so hygiene was non-existent. Elderly women looked after the children, together with a few mothers in their last months of pregnancy and those who had recently given birth. The children were fed rice soup with a little salt. While they slept the women wove palm leaf mats, or sewed clothes. Elderly women who were still agile and in good health had to help in the fields, together with everyone else.

In each hamlet a large shed had been constructed where elderly men with special skills could be employed. There they made ropes, constructed fish traps, wove baskets, or forged simple agricultural implements. Others grew vegetable and tobacco seedlings. Still others were responsible for maintaining the water level in the rice fields by opening and closing paddy dykes, while younger men pedalled the irrigation wheels. A special job for the elderly from "new families" was the production of "number one manure". Human excrement was collected from the toilets of the hamlet and transported by ox cart to the grounds of the pagoda. There it was mixed with ash and fine earth made from ground termite hills, packed into bricks and allowed to dry in the sun. Once it was dry it was stored in the

Thumb-printing a marriage certificate.

Threshing rice at night.

pagoda for use in the rice paddies and gardens when needed. Those detailed to do this work could only obey: they had to be careful never to complain or express disgust.

Urine was also not allowed to go to waste. Each morning the young revolutionary nurses from the hospital collected the urine stored in jars outside every house and transported it to the village "pharmacy". There it was mixed with some crushed plants and poisonous seeds, before being distilled to obtain a kind of insecticide. Some batches of the concoction proved to be so potent that when it was used many plants died.

Some work was more pleasant, but was always reserved for "old people". This included making drugs in the pharmacy, boiling down palm sugar, and working in the kitchens. The cooks were responsible for going each day to the village storehouses to obtain rice, vegetables, dried fish (or sometimes fresh meat), salt and sugar for the day's meals. Quantities were determined by the member of the hamlet committee in charge of the economy. The cooks were assisted by four off-siders who worked in the dining hall, or gathered vegetables or fruit. They had the right to use bicycles to transport what was needed. Each day a special group was detailed to go fishing. They usually managed to catch about four kilograms of fish for each one hundred people eating that day. Fish was the staple protein, though occasionally when few were caught, some chickens might be requisitioned (all chickens were communally owned, though still cared for by each family; ducks were part of a single village flock). More often chickens and ducks were reserved for the meals of village officials. It was forbidden to kill an ox or a buffalo since these were needed for ploughing and transport, and for breeding after the losses inflicted by the war. The village had a piggery, near the kitchens, but pork was a luxury reserved for special occasions, such as the commemoration of the communist victory of 17 April 1975, or the anniversary of the founding of the Communist Party of Kampuchea. Except for such "festivals", however, and despite increased production, both the quantity and quality of food served in the communal dining hall declined during 1977.

Two other special duties had to be regularly performed: carting water and collecting firewood. Both usually fell to "new people" since they entailed hard work. Water had to be brought daily in buckets from the village pond to the tank outside the dining hall. Firewood came at first from around the hamlet, but after a number of large trees had been destroyed the authorities decreed that fuel should be obtained from further afield. A group of ten men was formed to go and cut timber in a forest area more

The timber-cutting detail.

Punishment to fit the "crime".

than thirty kilometres away for two months at a time. "Old people" did not want to be away from their families for such a long period, so married men from "new families" were usually chosen to go. After Bun was married he fell into this category, and was detailed to join a timber cutting group. He did not mind this work as a change, for the food was more plentiful. They had sufficient rice, fish were abundant, and there were many wild edible plants in the forest. Whereas in the communal dining room one small smoked fish might be served for eight people, in the forest workers had one each.

Each day each man was expected to cut two cubic metres of firewood. If he failed to do so, he would be criticized at the evening meeting by the Khmer Rouge group leaders and his fellow wood cutters. Sometimes they had to cut timber in a flooded section of the forest. This was particularly dangerous since venomous snakes were common, mosquitoes collected in swarms, and the men feared malaria. Bun heard reports that in some places wood cutters had been blown up by bombs left undetonated after the war, but no-one from Maesor Prachan was killed or injured in this way. The timber was cut with axes and machetes, and stacked ready for carting to the village. The work was heavy, but the good food made up for it.

In one part of the forest where the Phum Andong group went to cut timber, they came upon a very poor village where the people were much worse off than at Maesor Prachan. Before the war they had grown maize and vegetables, but not rice; they had traded their surplus corn for rice. But when the Khmer Rouge abolished both markets and money, and forbade the movement of people and goods between villages, trade was no longer possible and the villagers had been forced to clear more forest and attempt to construct their own paddies. But the area was not suitable for rice; water was scarce, and the soil was poor. Most people were suffering from serious malnutrition, though Bun noticed that the village authorities and the local militia were well fed. He was surprised that the people of this village should have been in such a predicament, since they were overwhelmingly "old people" to whom the Khmer Rouge were usually more sympathetic. But Angkar functioned in such a way as virtually to exclude exceptions of policy which might have alleviated hardships in special circumstances.

Malnutrition, and actual starvation, were not uncommon even in 1977, when agricultural production country-wide had significantly increased, since no machinery had been established to supply villages where crops had failed. People living in the rice-growing area of the Eastern Zone were relatively lucky in this respect, a fact that was brought home to Bun by the plight of the forest village. He heard rumours of places where, in desperation, starving villagers had secretly killed their oxen for food, against the dictates of Angkar. As a punishment those guilty had been harnessed to ploughs or harrows themselves, and forced to pull them until they collapsed and died. Such rumours were not uncommon, and served as the only source of information, in the absence of any real news, on conditions in others part of the country. But no rumours reached Maesor Prachan of the struggle for power within the CPK which by then was already threatening the very foundations of the regime.

CHAPTER 7

Factions and Purges

When the CPK took power in April 1975, it was a deeply fragmented party. During the course of the war, the virtually independent Zone Party Committees had become geographical power bases for groups of revolutionaries of differing backgrounds, with different political experiences, and with differing views on the kind of Kampuchean socialism they wished to create and the best way to go about it. Agreement was limited to the need to transform the social and economic basis of Kampuchean society, and recognition that Vietnam posed the likeliest threat to Kampuchean independence.

But as the discussion which took place at the "Special Centre Assembly" on 17 April 1975 conclusively demonstrated, there was little agreement on what means to adopt in tackling these problems. Even decisions that were taken could often not be enforced. Although the Politburo was in the hands of Pol Pot and his close supporters, its authority was limited. The Party Centre might decide upon an internal policy of radical socialization and an external one of uncompromising confrontation with Vietnam, but that was no guarantee that these would be either universally accepted within the Party, or uniformly enforced throughout the country. For the Party Centre, therefore, a primary aim during the first eighteen months following victory was to unify the Party and ensure Party discipline. But though Pol Pot's radical nationalist faction was in a majority in the Politburo, they still represented a minority within the Party as a whole. The means they chose to enforce their will was not reasoned discussion leading to a majority vote, but the Stalinist method of terror — enforcement of unquestioning obedience through the threat of arrest, torture, and execution. Their willingness to use such methods was dramatically demonstrated by the early arrest and subsequent secret execution of the popular and charismatic revolutionary leader Hou Youn, purportedly for his outspoken opposition to Pol Pot's policy of evacuating the cities and abolishing markets and money.[1]

The radical nationalist group consisted of a core of former student revolutionaries who had learned their ideological Marxism in France. In addition to Pol Pot these included notably Ieng Sary (married to Pol Pot's sister-in-law), Son Sen and Vorn Veth (who fell out with the group in 1978). Khieu Samphan, a lesser figure in the CPK, came increasingly to be identified with this group; but more important, the tough peasant revolutionary Ta Mok, who seized power in the Southwest Zone in 1973, also supported the Pol Pot faction. Another supporter was Nuon Chea, Deputy Secretary-General of the Party, responsible for the training of Party cadres. Together with Son Sen, who was in charge of the Party's Military Cadre Training School, Nuon Chea provided a steady stream of well-indoctrinated radical nationalist cadres as replacements for those purged. Most importantly, the Party Centre also controlled the State Security apparatus which operated from headquarters at Tuol Sleng prison on the outskirts of Phnom Penh under the command of an ex-schoolteacher known only as Deuch, a former trusted lieutenant of Ta Mok.

Although the radical nationalists lacked the clear majority necessary to enforce their policies on the Party in 1975, they were in an excellent position to strengthen their control over the Party and to undermine, and finally destroy, their opponents.[2] The resistance to their radical programme encountered by the Pol Pot group in 1975 convinced them of the need to act quickly so as to minimize opposition. In the estimation of the radical nationalists, time was short. A leisurely process of social transformation would not create rapidly enough a strong and unified Kampuchea capable of withstanding Vietnamese blandishments. The longer their policies took to implement, the more opportunities would present themselves for the Vietnamese to interfere in Kampuchea. In fact a suspicion seems quickly to have taken root that those who adopted delaying tactics might be doing so for ulterior motives, and might already be acting for the Vietnamese.

One set of opponents of the radical nationalists during 1975 and 1976 were those whom Ben Kiernan has called the "Cultural Revolution Group". They included Hu Nim and Phouk Chhay, formerly active in the Kampuchea-China Friendship Association, Tiv Ol, an associate of Hu Nim, and the Northern Zone Party Secretary Koy Thuon, who was also on good terms with Pol Pot. The Cultural Revolution Group agreed on the need for a rapid and radical socio-economic transformation of Kampuchean society, and recognized Vietnam as the "acute enemy" of Kampuchea, but they favoured the "mass democracy" of the Chinese Cultural Revolution as the best means by which to mobilize the Kampuchean people for the great national task which faced them. They believed, too, that the welfare of the masses could not be ignored if their revolutionary potential was to be tapped. The Cultural Revolution group thus opposed not the ends, but the means employed by the radical nationalists. They objected to the Stalinist methods of the latter, their use of the Party as a means of repression to control the masses rather than to mobilize their enthusiastic support. But political participation of the masses was precisely what the radical nationalists feared would both lead to their own demise, and provide opportunities for Vietnam to intervene in Kampuchean affairs.

The second major group opposed to the radical nationalists may be called the "Party Veterans". Most of these were former Khmer Issarak insurgents who had remained in Kampuchea instead of regrouping in North Vietnam. Some, such as Nhim Ros and So Phim, Zone Secretaries in the Northwest and East respectively, had remained underground. Others, including Non Suon, Chow Chet and Keo Meas, had formed the Pracheachon Party to contest elections against Sihanouk's Sangkum Party. In 1963 most of the Pracheachon leaders were arrested and imprisoned until Sihanouk's overthrow in 1970 when they were released and joined the maquis. As a group these men, while acquiescing in the elimination of most of the Khmer Vietminh and recognizing Vietnam as a long-term threat to Kampuchean independence, had developed, as a result of their previous contacts, not a liking for the Vietnamese, but a respect for the methods and goals of Vietnamese communism. Most favoured a similar approach to Kampuchean problems. But this was enough for them to be seen by the radical nationalists as a potential fifth column within the CPK through whom Vietnamese influence could be exercised. It would be a mistake, however, to see the Party Veterans as pro-Vietnamese. They seem to have favoured "normal" relations with Vietnam in order for the Khmer revolution not to be diverted from its proper path, the building of socialism in Kampuchea. But they were not, as a group, stooges for Vietnam. That some may have been forced into seeking Vietnamese support through their opposition to Pol Pot was largely due to the fanaticism of the radical nationalists themselves.

For the next three years, until the complete victory of the radical nationalists by mid-1978, these three groups within the CPK struggled for political power. In 1975, the geographical balance of power was approximately as follows. The radical nationalists at the Party Centre controlled directly only the Northeast Zone. In addition they wielded considerable influence in the Northern Zone, in the Special Region around Phnom Penh and in the city itself, and in the Southwest, where Ta Mok was an ally but where members of both the other groups were still influential in the upper levels of the Party structure. The Cultural Revolution group was concentrated in Phnom Penh, where its intellectual leaders were members of the government, and in the Southwest, where, however, their followers were progressively replaced by cadres loyal to Ta Mok. Both the Eastern and Northwestern Zones were in the hands of Party Veterans, but the two areas were well separated from each other, and contact and cooperation between the Eastern and Northwestern Zones seems to have been minimal.

In July 1976, an important move was made to centralize political power with the announcement of formation of a unified Kampuchean Revolutionary Army (KRA). This meant not that regional forces under Zone control were disbanded but that henceforth the training of central KRA units and appointment of political officers would be the prerogative of the CPK Central Committee. These loyal military units could, and later would, be used to put down any armed opposition to the Party Centre by Zone forces loyal to deposed regional leaders.

The centralization of political control over the army, and the consequent weakening of regional power bases, should be seen in the context of the factional manoeuvring within the CPK that gained momentum during 1976. In September, Pol Pot stepped down as Prime Minister, to be replaced by Nuon Chea. This may have been a tactical move, though it seems more likely that it was engineered by a coalition of Pol Pot's opponents within the Party.

Much happened in Kampuchea over the next three weeks. Important policy changes were put into effect which reflected a retreat from the radical economic self-sufficiency practised until then. The first Kampuchean trade delegation left for Albania, Yugoslavia and North Korea; rubber exports began to Singapore and Thailand; and enquiries were made for the purchase overseas of medical supplies and anti-malarial spraying equipment.

Meanwhile Pol Pot returned to his power base in the Northeast where he is reported to have personally directed an intensive purge and associated re-education programme among Party and Army cadres. This "political rectification" campaign was later extended to the Northern Zone, and then to the Northwest. Its aim was to install Party cadres not merely committed to the radical nationalist line, but personally loyal to Pol Pot.

In early October 1976, the Chinese Gang of Four were arrested and the eclipse of the radicals in China seems to have undermined the position of the Cultural Revolution group in Kampuchea. Kampuchea could look only to China for support against Vietnam; it was essential for the leadership of the CPK to be on good terms with the new Chinese leadership. We do not know what shifting alliances were responsible for the return to power of Pol Pot. The first public indication that he was again heading the government of Democratic Kampuchea was a savage denunciation of the "Gang of Four anti-Party clique" on 22 October, signed simply "Pol Pot: Prime Minister".

Pol Pot's return was the signal for a concerted high-level purge of members of rival factions. The first targets were leaders of the Veterans group, in particular those whose geographical power base was the Northwest Zone. Two senior cadres (Keo Moni and Non Suon) were immediately arrested.

Then in the first half of 1977 a series of purges broke the power of both the Veterans in the Northwest and the Cultural Revolution Group. Young Southwest Zone cadres, chosen from among the poorest peasant families and trained in the radical-nationalist-controlled Party Cadre School, were sent to purge lower level cadres in the Northwest Zone. Meanwhile two senior government ministers — Touch Phoeun (Public Health) and Sua Doeum (Trade) — identified with the Veteran faction were arrested and sent for interrogation to Tuol Sleng prison. At the same time leaders of the Cultural Revolution group and their supporters were being picked off. Koy Thuon, Party Secretary of the Northern Zone, was arrested on 25 January 1977, to be followed a month later by most of the top cadres of the Siemreap Special Region. Then in succession the major leaders of the Cultural Revolution faction Phouk Chhay (14 March), Hu Nim (10 April), and Tiv Ol (6 June) were arrested to be tortured in Tuol Sleng and eventually executed. The last major Veteran leader in the Northwest, Nhim Ros, apparently joined armed insurgents fighting

Central Army troops before being captured and executed in March 1978.

The purges carried out in the North and Northwest were fanatically thorough. Cadres down to the hamlet level were not simply replaced as before, but executed. Military units under Zone control were also purged of all officers and political cadres. But despite the thoroughness and secrecy with which the purges were conducted (victims were invited to celebrations, or for discussions on Party policy, and simply disappeared), armed uprisings broke out in both the North and Northwest between February and August 1977. These were put down by Central Army troops, with the mass execution of entire units of rebels. Resistance spluttered on in some areas, however, until the arrival of the Vietnamese eighteen months later.

Two things are remarkable about the purges which took place from October 1976 to the second half of 1977. The first is that they were accompanied by a rising tide of conflict along the border with Vietnam, creating a sense of national emergency and added political tension. The second is that those purged were consistently identified as foreign agents: their crime was treason.

It seems likely that fighting with Vietnam was deliberately provoked by the radical nationalists in command of the KRA, both in order to heighten internal tension, and thus provide an excuse in terms of national security for the arrests being carried out; and to prevent Vietnam from aiding or making contact with any of those marked down to be purged. But border conflict with Vietnam was also part of a deliberate policy to counter what the radical nationalists saw as Vietnam's aggressive expansionism. An Eastern Zone Conference was reportedly told in July 1977:

> "We must continue to be on guard and be prepared to do battle with and smash the enemy . . . If the enemy commits aggression . . . we must cross into and stop and smash him right on his own land. This is intended to further increase his difficulties . . . He will no longer dare to repeat his aggression against us; rather it will be his turn to strain to stop us.[3]

All opposition to the policies of the Central Committee was by this time interpreted as evidence of foreign subversion. The "three-fold elimination" used as a slogan within the Party during this period was aimed at ridding Kampuchea of agents of the CIA, the KGB, and the Vietnamese revisionists and expansionists. But a party directive made clear that the *real* targets were all those believed to be under Vietnamese influence who disagreed with radical nationalist policies.

By the end of 1977, the only region over which the Central Committee did not exercise total control was the Eastern Zone, which remained under the leadership of the veteran So Phim. The Eastern Zone consisted of that part of the country east of the Mekong River and south of the former province of Kratie. It contained in its five regions a population of about 1.8 millions. Because of its strategic importance for the southern Vietnamese insurgency, both before and after 1954, Vietnamese influence in the Eastern Zone had always been greater than in other parts of Kampuchea. This did not mean there was any real affection for the Vietnamese among most Eastern Zone cadres, but contacts over the years had encouraged a more realistic appreciation of the strengths and weaknesses of the Vietnamese, and a greater readiness to profit from contact with them.

Partly in response to the influence of Vietnamese communism, Eastern Zone cadres played a significant role in the development of the Kampuchean communist movement. In the struggle against the French, something like half the active insurgents of the Khmer Issarak were concentrated in the Eastern Zone area. As a young peasant activist, So Phim had commanded Issarak forces in Svay Rieng province, the Parrot's Beak which thrusts into the southern Vietnamese delta. At the 1963 congress of the Communist Party of Kampuchea, So Phim stood against Pol Pot for the position of secretary-general of the Party. The position went to the French-trained intellectual, but So Phim gained fourth position in the Politburo, and was seen as a continuing threat to the political dominance of the returned students. Perhaps in order to deprive him of influence at the Party Centre, So Phim was given "special responsibility" for the Eastern Zone.

During the 1960s So Phim concentrated on building up the CPK organization in the Eastern Zone. He was reportedly unhappy at Vietnamese support for Sihanouk, and the refusal of Hanoi to provide the Khmer Rouge with arms, but he took advantage of Vietnamese assistance in training Kampuchean cadres. He also made full use of those veteran Khmer activists from Issarak days who, like himself, had cooperated closely with the Vietminh against the French, but who had not gone to North Vietnam in 1954. Among these veteran activists was Chhien, chief of Region 22 in which Maesor Prachan was situated. But So Phim always maintained his independence from the Vietnamese. Armed struggle began in the Eastern Zone in 1968, despite the lack of Vietnamese assistance, and in the face of their active disapproval. When fighting with government forces went against the insurgents in 1969, the Khmer insurgents used the border as did the Vietnamese — they crossed into Vietnam and demanded sanctuary in communist-controlled areas. The Vietnamese reluctantly agreed, but made sure their guests stayed well away from the frontier so as not to jeopardize Hanoi's relations with Sihanouk. When Sihanouk was overthrown in 1970, So Phim's political and military cadres were well prepared to take advantage of the new situation.

During the war from 1970 to 1975 the Eastern Zone was run by a Party Committee consisting of So Phim, his deputy Phuong, the Zone military commander, the Party Secretaries of the five regions, and the head of the Zone administrative office. In 1970 they had under their command only about 300 fully-armed guerrillas, but this number increased rapidly as Vietnamese forces drove back Lon Nol's troops, and turned large areas of eastern Kampuchea over to the administration of the Zone Party Committee. However, relations with the Vietnamese deteriorated over Hanoi's decision to negotiate a cease-fire with the U.S. The Eastern Zone suffered like the rest of Kampuchea from massive U.S. bombing. Distrust, followed by bitter denunciation of Vietnam, led to elimination of the Khmer Vietminh veterans. Ten veterans working in the Eastern Zone were killed in 1973, and the remaining sixty-one were arrested in August 1974 and made to perform forced agricultural labour in Region 21. All but one, who managed to escape to Vietnam, were later murdered. Anti-Vietnamese feelings were reflected in the Party history published in the Eastern Zone in September 1973 which specifically denounced the Vietnamese "game of negotiations". While it acknowledged Vietnamese support in the past, it clearly favoured the independent pursuit of Kampuchean interests.

The events of 1973 and 1974, the rigours of the struggle against Lon Nol, and mounting hatred of the Vietnamese, had the effect of bringing the communist movement in the Eastern Zone more into line with the radical-nationalist policies espoused by the Party Centre. Differences remained, however, though in time of war these were prevented from becoming pronounced by the common need to put military matters first. The failure of Eastern Zone cadres to implement the same harsh recruitment programme, iron discipline, and forced relocation of population that occurred, for example, in the North and Northwest, could be justified by the necessity not to alienate the peasantry and undermine the war effort. But once peace had been won, there

121

was less excuse for not putting Centre policies into effect.

Disagreement soon arose, however, over how rapidly radical policies for the socialist transformation of Kampuchea should be implemented, and over how aggressive Kampuchea should be towards Vietnam. Differences over these two broad policy areas not only soured relations between the Party Centre and the Eastern Zone committee, but, more damaging still, split the Zone leadership itself. Towards the end of 1975, reorganization of the Eastern Party Committee saw Chan, the ambitious and ruthless Party secretary of Region 21, elevated with Centre backing to the rank of Zone deputy secretary, second only to So Phim. For the following two years Chan actively supported the radical nationalist line, first by replacing lower level cadres with men loyal to himself, then by progressively eliminating senior cadres opposed to Centre policies. He was assisted in this by the disbanding of those Eastern Zone security forces directly under the control of Zone Party Secretary So Phim, and their reorganization under the State Security apparatus. Because regional and district security forces continued to operate, however, regional Party Secretaries still had the power to arrest virtually whomsoever they pleased. This left Chan, in Region 21, free to carry out purges of any lower level cadres he considered unsympathetic towards the Centre's radical nationalist policies.

The purges which began towards the end of 1976 had their effect in the Eastern Zone. The increased strength of the Party Centre led to belated implementation of Centre policies, such as communal dining, which until then had been resisted. Some cadres, including Yon, the hamlet chief of Phum Andong, were replaced. Local security forces from Chan's Region 21 began arresting "pro-Vietnamese" cadres and handing them over to the State Security apparatus for interrogation in Tuol Sleng. There, under torture, they implicated others in alleged networks of opposition to Central Party policy. These names were then sent to the Eastern Zone Party Committee for action. But as many of those so implicated were veteran Party members, personally known to So Phim as dedicated revolutionaries, he was reluctant to take action against them. This increased the suspicion of Pol Pot and his circle that So Phim might himself be involved in what appeared to them from the distorted and incredible confessions they were sent from Tuol Sleng to be a widespread Vietnamese-backed conspiracy to engineer their overthrow. Increasingly, therefore, they relied upon Chan, who was empowered to extend his purges into Regions 23 and 24. During 1977 as many as half of all regional and district level cadres were replaced (as was Eak, village chief of Maesor Prachan), arrested, or murdered.

In this way great damage was done to the Party in the Eastern Zone, particularly at the district level where many veteran Party leaders were killed and replaced by young fanatics personally loyal to Chan rather than to the Zone Party Committee headed by So Phim. Ben Kiernan estimates that as many as a thousand Eastern Zone cadres were eliminated during 1976 and 1977, preparing the way for the final military seizure of power by the Party Centre in May 1978. Many others fled to Vietnam, thus confirming them as traitors in the eyes of the radical nationalists, and providing them with further proof of the need to continue the purges. Those who retained their posts were naturally under severe pressure to implement the Centre's harsher policies.

Two moves prepared the way for the eventual fall of So Phim. The first was the replacement noted above of local Eastern Zone cadres by young cadres from the Southwest; the second was the enforcement of Central control over Eastern Zone army units. During the civil war from 1970 to 1975, local forces had been recruited and trained in the Eastern Zone. They were commanded by military cadres from the same area for whom they had developed a degree of personal loyalty. Eastern Zone forces owed their immediate political allegiance to the Zone Party Committee, and thus provided powerful support for the Zone Party secretary. In the East, many military commanders felt a personal allegiance towards So Phim. To be successful, therefore, any move by the Centre against So Phim had first to neutralize these regional loyalties.

Of the five brigades operating in the East by April 1975, two were transferred to Central control as part of the reorganization of the army and were raised to divisions. In May 1976 the commanding officer of one (the 170th) was arrested, probably on suspicion of being party to a plot on Pol Pot's life. Under torture he implicated officers of the division's 3rd Brigade, many of whom were purged. Other brigade officers escaped attention, however, including the officer commanding the 4th Brigade, one Heng Samrin. Thus at the end of 1976, Eastern Zone forces still remained largely intact. But the border fighting against Vietnam which began in earnest early in 1977 necessitated the despatch of additional troops under Central command, notably from the Southwest. These were then ideally positioned to be used to purge remaining units with Eastern Zone loyalties.

By mid-1977 four Kampuchean divisions were involved in the border fighting with Vietnam, though with a certain lack of enthusiasm on the part of some Eastern Zone commanders, who believed such attacks to be counter-productive. After certain units failed to respond to orders to attack across the border, numbers of military cadres began to be secretly purged and executed.

The fighting with Vietnam gave the Centre the excuse it needed to set up a new military command structure in the East. Military action was organized on two fronts: a southern front down Highway 1 into the Parrot's Beak area; and a northern front along Highway 7 towards the Vietnamese town of An Loc. So Phim was named President of the "Front Committee" coordinating these military moves, but with Pauk, Party Secretary of the Central Zone as his deputy. The radical nationalists thus managed to place one of their leading supporters at the heart of the Eastern Zone Party apparatus. During the second half of 1977 So Phim's power was further undermined while he was away in Beijing for two months' medical treatment. He returned to find the Highway 7 front under Pauk's direct command, with responsibility for the Highway 1 front in the hands of Pol Pot's trusted Defence Minister, Son Sen.

On 24 September, Son Sen's forces struck deep into Southern Vietnam, northeast and southwest from the Parrot's Beak salient. Before being forced to withdraw, Kampuchean troops carried out an horrific indiscriminate massacre of Vietnamese civilians. Men, women and children were beaten, raped and slaughtered in a way which defies all understanding. Teenage soldiers (yotheas) conditioned for years to hate and kill, inured to cruelty and the infliction of pain, did what they had been trained to do — kill Vietnamese! Ben Kiernan recounts that one company commander was so sickened and horrified by what he had seen his own troops do that, when he returned to Kampuchea, he wrote a note to his junior officers and shot himself.

In December 1977, the Vietnamese retaliated by invading and occupying for about a month a number of border areas in Kampuchea. During the invasion, Khmer dissidents who had already fled to Vietnam made attempts to contact leading Eastern Zone cadres, but apparently without success. Kampuchean forces retreated in disarray, amid considerable pillage and looting, though which troops were mainly responsible remains unclear. Kampuchea rejected Vietnamese calls for a negotiated settlement, broke off diplomatic relations with Hanoi, and mounted a concerted counter-attack. However, when Vietnamese forces withdrew in early January 1978, this was a voluntary move: the Kampuchean army in the East was in the throes of yet another upheaval.

Even as the Vietnamese invasion was underway, the purges continued. Commanders who had retreated in the face of the Vietnamese thrust were accused of treachery. At the end of December 1977 the head of Chan's security forces was killed in a shoot-out with troops loyal to an Eastern Zone commander he had personally just executed. This seems to have convinced the Party Centre that resistance in the Eastern Zone was so widespread that the total eradication of all opposition would be necessary. This could only be done through a military takeover of the region by loyal forces from other areas, notably the Central and Southwestern Zones, and a total purge of all political and military cadres in any way connected with the man by now held responsible for all opposition in the East, So Phim himself.

By early 1978 So Phim had been dropped from the Politburo to be replaced by Son Sen. Purges of both political and military cadres continued in areas of the East under control of Central or Southwestern Zone forces, and even of some cadres from those other zones thought to have been influenced by contact with Eastern Zone cadres. Action in the East may have been delayed, however, by the discovery of a planned military uprising in western Kampuchea. This was foiled by the arrest, imprisonment and execution of local Party officials, but the Centre was forced to act quickly to strengthen its control over the army in other Zones, thus precipitating another series of purges. Other rebellions, notably in parts of the Northern Zone, also had to be dealt with.

By April 1978 the Party Centre was ready to move in the East. By then ten times as many prisoners from the East were being held in Tuol Sleng as from any other zone. Under torture they were implicating other cadres so fast that the Centre could hardly keep up with the necessary purges. Even as fighting continued with Vietnam, officers in all Eastern Zone military units were being executed right down to the level of platoon leaders. Simultaneously a propaganda offensive urged soldiers to take the war into Vietnam and recapture Kampuchea Krom (the southern Vietnamese delta). Troops were told that two million Kampucheans, "pure and hard", had only to kill thirty Vietnamese each to remove for ever the threat Vietnam allegedly posed to the national existence of Kampuchea. Each Kampuchean soldier had only to fill his quota!

Phiny's sisters are arrested.

In the East, a fresh round of purges of Party cadres down to the hamlet level followed the final defeat of So Phim, and the failure of a last-ditch military rebellion by troops loyal to him. But even when the Party Centre had finally gained control over the entire country, the killing did not stop. In the diseased imagination of the Centre leadership virtually every Kampuchean living in the Eastern Zone was suspected of being contaminated by the pro-Vietnamese virus which had supposedly affected all purged cadres. In particular, "new people" were assumed to be infected: all were seen as potential traitors who might undermine the national crusade against Vietnam.

Throughout the Eastern Zone, however, people knew nothing of the power struggle that was being played out inside Angkar itself. Nothing was gained from the point of view of the villagers when one set of cadres was replaced by another. Yet in 1978 the villages of Eastern Kampuchea, including Maesor Prachan, became caught up in the fratricidal strife that was tearing apart the CPK, with results which none of their inhabitants could ever have imagined.

CHAPTER 8

Final Solution in the East

The destructive struggle for power within the Kampuchean Communist Party, and deteriorating relations with Vietnam during 1977, set the scene for the tragic events of 1978 in the Eastern Zone. During the Vietnamese offensive of December 1977 which penetrated deeply into Kampuchean border areas, the sound of heavy artillery could be heard in Maesor Prachan. But people there were told nothing of what was happening — only that the Khmer army was teaching the Vietnamese annexationists a lesson, and would soon occupy Prey Nokor (formerly the Khmer name for Saigon).[1]

The purges and border fighting during 1977 affected Maesor Prachan only indirectly, but radical policies were progressively more harshly enforced. Throughout the Eastern Zone, cadres began arresting every remaining Vietnamese resident and anyone who, through family connections, could be suspected of harbouring friendly feelings towards Vietnam. In Phum Andong an old Vietnamese woman aged about seventy married to a Kampuchean peasant was arrested and carted off to the district gaol at Snaypol to be killed. Anyone could be arrested for using a language other than Khmer, a rule which applied even in private and which affected mostly Chinese and Chams.

This strict and harsh application of Khmer Rouge rules and regulations extended to the cadres themselves. Early in 1978,

Prak, the hamlet chief of Phum Andong, was purged for what would earlier have been considered a relatively minor offence. His downfall came about after he tried to cover up the rape of a Chinese girl by two of his spies. The girl and her family had been arrested for speaking Chinese together. All were beaten, and the girl raped in Prak's presence. The two culprits were later denounced to the district authorities through the help of district spies known to the family. Both hamlet spies implicated Prak under torture, and the hamlet chief was arrested and charged with both failure to discipline his cadres and corruption — the ordering of specially prepared food. To general rejoicing, which everyone was careful to hide, Prak was incarcerated in Peareang jail. By this time he was excessively fat and so became a favourite target for torture because in appearance he resembled a district governor under the former regime. He was eventually executed just prior to the overthrow of So Phim.

By late 1977 the new and harsher policies in force throughout the Eastern Zone were being felt in Maesor Prachan. There was a new wave of arrests of any "new people" suspected of being half-hearted in their support for the Khmer Rouge, anyone with political connections with the former regime, or anyone who might welcome the overthrow of the Pol Pot regime, even by Vietnam. All those arrested were taken to Peareang gaol to be re-educated. Many prisoners from other parts of the district passed through Maesor Prachan. They included a few remaining former government soldiers (all officers had long since been executed), teachers, civil servants, and students whose commitment to the new regime was suspect. All were accused publicly of being agents of the CIA, the KGB, or the Vietnamese — often all three at once! Among those arrested were Bun's cousin, Mom Khunna, who had lived with the Ung family while at school in Phnom Penh from 1971 to 1975. He had come to the attention of village cadres when he was sick but seen to be eating well. Despite frantic pleas that Mom had only been a student, district cadres accused him of being a former soldier, and took him away.

The most terrible experience for Bun and Phiny, however, came on 7 December 1977 when two of Phiny's sisters were arrested, one charged with being a member of Lon Nol's force of girl commandos, the other with having been married to a Lon Nol officer. The grounds for accusing Somalee of being a commando were that hamlet cadres had found a photograph showing her in army uniform the previous year during their search of the Kang's house at the time communal dining was introduced. The photograph had shown Somalee and some of her friends in the high school cadet corps, but she had never joined the army. Earlier in the year she had been married, and at the time of her arrest was three month's pregnant. Phiny's other sister, Amara, had been married to a young lieutenant killed while fighting in 1970 and was apparently arrested on these grounds alone. She and her six-year-old daughter lived with Bun and Phiny. Amara and Somalee were then aged twenty-seven and twenty-five.

Arrests in 1978 were made in broad daylight, for everyone to witness. The black-clad district security militia used to come from Peareang by bicycle when only one or two people were to be arrested and their very presence in the village brought fear. No-one knew who would be next to be accused. The day Phiny's sisters were arrested the Khmer Rouge brought a horse and cart into the village. It was dusk. The girls had their hands tied tightly behind their backs. Their faces were white with fear. Bun's mother-in-law pleaded to see her daughters, but permission was refused. Neither she nor Bun could do anything: to have argued in the girls' favour would have led to their own immediate arrest. Any demonstration of their torment and sorrow would have been taken as reflecting unrevolutionary attitudes. They could only stand, staring into the darkness as the two girls and one other prisoner were driven away to the district gaol. None was ever seen again. Later Bun was to discover for himself the appalling conditions under which they must have died.

In December 1977 thousands of workers from Maesor Prachan were mobilized to build a great dam across the Tonle Toch before the next wet season. This was the largest project Bun had worked on. Teams of married men and women together with mobile brigades from Maesor Prachan and other villages, numbering perhaps 20,000 workers in all, toiled for five months to complete the dam. The construction was of earth fill, eighty metres long and forty metres thick, wide enough for eight trucks to drive across abreast. This massive project near the hamlet of Phum Prek Champa, eight kilometres from Phum Andong, ex-hausted the energies of the village. During construction no rest days were permitted. Work was continuous, for up to fifteen hours a day with hardly a day's break. The dam withstood the unusually high floods of 1978, but was never repaired, and was subsequently breached and washed away by the floods of the following year.

Construction of the Tonle Toch dam was part of an overall plan to rationalize agriculture and irrigation in Peareang district. In 1976 rice paddies had been reformed into regular

"Surplus" rice being loaded onto Khmer Rouge lorries.

The way the Tonle Toch dam was planned.

Construction of the Tonle Toch dam.

100-metre squares. The following year irrigation canals had been built. In 1978 dams were constructed to direct water into the waiting canals. The flow of water in the Tonle Toch even in the dry season made construction difficult. Pylons were first driven into the river bed and a bamboo net stretched between them. Fill of stone and brick was dumped along the upstream side of the net, to be followed by more rocks and dirt. At first some fill was transported by boat, but as the dam crept out from the bank on either side, all additional fill was carried by land from an enormous square pit dug in the paddies just beyond Prek Champa hamlet.

As the dam progressed it became necessary to draw off water, via spillways on each side into already constructed canals. The spillway incorporated sluice gates to control the volume of water but the cadre in charge of the project had never built such a spillway. He sketched the plan to be followed with a stick in the sand. Two pylons on either side were to hold the sluice gates, but the pylons collapsed. A new plan was drawn, but that too failed. Eventually the project supervisor was sent to Battambang province to see how a similar spillway had been constructed there. When he came back, work went ahead, but the spillway never functioned properly.

The planning and construction of the spillway, and weakness in the dam itself, illustrated the amateurism of such projects. No civil engineer was involved, for Western science and technology were condemned as bourgeois learning. Trained Kampuchean engineers were Western-educated enemies to be exterminated. Those who survived like Pin Yathay did so because they hid their identities.[2] Major dams were constructed on the same principles as small ones across minor streams, without the use of theodolites or other instruments and by men with little or no technical training who learned as they went. Practical knowledge gained on the job, through trial and error, was prized above anything to be found in books. Such knowledge was "pure", and Kampuchean, owing nothing to foreign initiatives or findings. Tragically, however, it could result in massive wasted effort. In some places water failed to flow in irrigation canals with insufficient gradient; in others dams were washed away — sometimes with serious loss of life.

Another project ordered at this time was the complete demolition of all pagodas and other places of worship. The Catholic cathedral in Phnom Penh was dismantled, stone by stone, until not even the foundations remained. The old pagoda in Phum Andong was also demolished. The broken bricks were used

The demolition of the Phum Andong pagoda.

as fill for the Tonle Toch dam, while the timber was stacked for building accommodation for mobile brigades and communal dining rooms. Only the pagoda in Phum Kompong Trea where Bun had been married was not destroyed as it was used as a storehouse for communal food supplies.

The only relief from work on the Tonle Toch dam site came with the third anniversary of the Khmer Rouge victory, the most important event of the year in Democratic Kampuchea. A three-day holiday was declared, during which compulsory mass meetings were held to hear speeches by Party leaders on the successes of the Revolution and policies for the future, notably victory over Vietnam. In the evening there was entertainment on a scale not previously seen in Maesor Prachan, including films and live performances. One of the films, titled simply "Democratic Kampuchea", lauded the achievements of the regime. It also showed high ranking members of the CPK, led by Pol Pot, welcoming a delegation from China. Some in the audience who knew him recognized Pol Pot as Saloth Sar. Although he was not so identified, this was the first time, three years after the founding of Democratic Kampuchea, that the people of Maesor Prachan realized who Pol Pot was, and the first time they had seen the collective leadership of the Khmer Rouge.

To Bun and his friends, starved as they had been of any entertainment for three years, the live performances were spectacular. They consisted of dancing, singing, short plays, and music, all of a properly revolutionary nature. But none had anything in common with traditional Khmer art forms; in fact to Bun the revolutionary songs and music seemed more Chinese, even Vietnamese, than Khmer.

In May 1978, factional dissension in the CPK reached its climax. The first that the people of Maesor Prachan knew of this internal struggle, however, was when So Phim was finally ousted. On 25 May a convoy of army jeeps and small cars drove through Maesor Prachan from Snaypol. In the lead vehicle were So Phim and members of his family accompanied by bodyguards and a number of higher Zone cadres (including Chhien, Party secretary of Region 22 who had had a large house built in Maesor Prachan, and Daok Samol, chief of Peareang district). Bun, who saw the vehicles pass, thought So Phim looked sad and distracted.

Though no-one in Maesor Prachan knew it at the time, the convoy made for Prek Pou on the Mekong where So Phim vainly tried to negotiate with Pol Pot and other members of the Central Committee to counter the forces arrayed against him. But on 3

The third anniversary celebrations in Maesor Prachan.

June Revolutionary Army troops came north from Phnom Penh to arrest him. So Phim committed suicide rather than be taken to the torture chambers of Tuol Sleng. That evening, as his wife and children prepared his body for burial, all were massacred and their corpses tossed into the river.[3]

In the turmoil of the following week, all civil order broke down in Maesor Prachan. Work was neglected and youths from the mobile brigades returned to their villages. Bun decided to take the risk of leaving Phum Andong without seeking permission, and go in search of his cousin and sisters-in-law at the district prison. He knew the gaol well. It was in what had formerly been the high school on the outskirts of Snaypol, fifteen kilometres from Phum Andong; he had passed it frequently when travelling to work sites with his comrades, and had seen prisoners working in its gardens. It seemed to him symbolic, in a country where all higher education and religious observance had been abolished, that in most districts schools and pagodas had become prisons and torture chambers.

When Bun and some "old people" who were also looking for arrested relatives arrived at the prison they found that all the prison guards had left, having killed every prisoner left in the gaol. Only the corpses remained and Bun was horrified. Many of the dead were in a pitiful state, mere skeletons that had been killed by blows with gun butts, strangled with scarves, or struck on the neck with machetes. The prison records were scattered everywhere, but there was no point in searching through them. Everyone Bun sought was dead, having either died in custody or been executed after confessing their "crimes". Everywhere was evidence of appalling conditions of filth and degradation, torture and humiliation. Prisoners were never simply arrested and shot: authorities had first to obtain the confessions which would justify their arrest, and thus confirm the omniscience and justice of Angkar in arresting them. Later Bun met up with two prisoners who had been working some distance from the gaol and had escaped the massacre. They told him that each prisoner was routinely deprived of food for two days upon arrival at the prison, and was then required to write out his or her confession. If it was not acceptable, it had to be done again. Prisoners were beaten or starved until they wrote what was demanded of them. A favourite torture was to pull out their fingernails with heavy pliers. Loudspeakers playing revolutionary music were turned up to drown out the screams. Each day prisoners were given less and less to eat until, weakened in body and spirit they succumbed to disease or were taken out and killed by a blow with a hoe or

The district prison.

axe to the back of the neck for the crimes to which they had by then confessed. Most common of these were that they had been spies for the Vietnamese, the CIA, or both. Their emaciated and broken bodies were buried in the prison grounds, and their dossiers neatly closed.

Bun could only imagine the agonies which Phiny's sisters had gone through. Prisoners had slept one against the other, their feet chained together and attached to the walls. They were forbidden to talk. Their toilet was an old ammunition box, and they urinated in jars. Anything spilt had to be wiped up. Food consisted of one meal of thin rice gruel and chopped cactus a day, even those prisoners with lesser crimes — "old people" who had committed some civil offence such as stealing for which confessions were not required — had had to work off their sentences in the prison garden before being released. Prisoners ate cockroaches, mice, anything they could catch. Many died of malnutrition and disease, and few who came to the prison left it again. The worst offenders were kept in an underground cage, hardly large enough for one man. When one occupant died, the next was forced into the cage and made to bury the body. Bun returned from Peareang sickened by the callousness and inhumanity of the regime. He had been deeply shocked by what he had seen, and for four years never told Phiny where he had been.

A few days after So Phim's flight, a helicopter flew over the village dropping leaflets accusing So Phim and his clique of being "traitors against the Communist Party of Kampuchea", and calling upon all cadres to return to their usual place of work. Most did so. Soon after, Revolutionary Army troops loyal to the Party Centre arrived in Peareang district. They came from the Southwest, hard-eyed, brutalized peasant boys who were strangers to the region and knew only how to obey orders. Discipline was quickly reimposed through a campaign of terror. Two of Phiny's brothers working in the Maesor Prachan mobile brigade were killed at this time, apparently as part of a deliberate policy of selective killing of "new people".

The new military authorities called upon all Eastern Zone troops to surrender and lay down their arms. Many did so, only to be promptly massacred. Others, hearing rumours of their likely fate, took to the jungle, or fled to Vietnam to swell the number of recruits joining the Vietnamese-organized Khmer resistance.

No troops were stationed in Maesor Prachan, but Bun heard the sounds of fighting in Snaypol. Later Southwest Zone army officers came to Maesor Prachan to inform people of the crimes of So Phim, and to tell them not to panic. Order had been restored.

The word of Angkar was to be obeyed. A week later all the Khmer Rouge cadres in Maesor Prachan were called upon to assemble in Phum Prek Champa hamlet to attend a meeting to discuss new policies. Once there they were arrested by Southwestern Zone soldiers, and tied up to be slaughtered at dusk with hoes, knives and axes. Some people from Phum Andong and more from Phum Prek Champa witnessed the massacre. Many more heard the screams of the victims. All were forced to dig their own shallow graves in scrub behind Chhien's house (Chhien himself was already a prisoner in Tuol Sleng). The girls were raped first. One named Pheng, a leader of the women's mobile group, was heard to shout before being killed: "Long live the Communist Party of Kampuchea". Another, Yim, screamed for justice. A soldier shouted "Here is your justice" as he struck her with a machete. In all about fifty people were killed: the chiefs and committee members of the village and each hamlet, the leader of the village mobile group, spies of the village security apparatus, even the doctors and nurses at the hospital. Later Bun saw one of the soldiers responsible for the killings jauntily wearing the scarf which had belonged to the head of the mobile group.

Everyone was happy that the executions had taken place; even "old people". It was as if a load had been lifted from people's shoulders. Those who had made life a misery for so long were dead; and everyone savoured the sweet taste of revenge. Similar scenes occurred in villages throughout the Eastern Zone. In some places villagers took the law into their own hands, and savagely killed Khmer Rouge cadres and their families. Cadres were hunted down, or succeeded in fleeing to the jungle. For the first time men began moving from village to village without passes. They carried rumours and reports of what was happening elsewhere which were eagerly listened to by people long starved of any news of events beyond their own village.

The Army officers explained that the executions had been necessary since it had been discovered that all those killed had been members of So Phim's traitorous clique. Secretly all had been working for a Vietnamese victory. It had been the duty of loyal soldiers to destroy the enemies of the Revolution. But, they explained, the executions must not be allowed to affect the functioning of the hamlet co-operatives. So for the next three weeks, until new cadres were appointed, each hamlet ran its own affairs in Maesor Prachan. Work continued, though not at the same previous intensity. The distinction between "old" and "new" families was, by common consent, allowed to lapse.

Towards the end of June, the military authorities sent a platoon of soldiers to Maesor Prachan, and appointed a new set of cadres. These were chosen from among the "old families" only. A three-day holiday was declared, which turned into a festival with the best food Bun could remember. After that the new chief was ordered to prepare a full census of all "new people" in the village but was not told why. Soon after the census had been completed a motorized river boat docked at Phum Yot hamlet. All "new families" in the hamlet were ordered to collect their belongings and board the boat. They were told only that Angkar had decided to move them to an area where there was more food — they were not told where. It was rumoured that they might be returning to Phnom Penh. Another rumour which no-one believed was that people moved from other villages away from the river were being taken off in ox carts and killed. Youths and girls were recalled from the mobile brigade and ordered to accompany their families. It was the height of the rainy season, and the annual flood was rising quickly. Ox carts were used to help some families move down to the river, for speed was essential.

Each day the boat made two trips, one at noon and a second in the evening, each time carrying as many as 150 men, women and children. It went downstream towards the district hospital, but soon returned for more passengers. It was obvious that they were not going far and was commonly believed that they were being transported some distance downstream to where a fleet of trucks was waiting on the opposite bank to take them to Phnom Penh.

It was not until the fourth day that reports began circulating about what was really happening. One of the deportees, Huor, had been a teacher living in Phum Maesor Prachan, and was a distant relative of Bun's. As the boat docked at dusk he had managed to slip away undetected, after his wife and two children had been led away. He returned to the village and reported that people were not being transported to Phnom Penh at all; they were being massacred at the district hospital.

Many refused to believe Huor, but Bun and two friends determined to find out for themselves. Under the new village cadres, rules were no longer as strict as before and movement from hamlet to hamlet was possible. But for three years people had been conditioned to obey without question: all initiative had been systematically crushed. No-one questioned Angkar: no-one asked why.

Bun and his two friends simply could not believe what they

Boarding the boat to the district hospital.

had been told. Not even the Khmer Rouge would butcher hundreds of men, women and children in cold blood. The next day, the fifth of the evacuation, the three companions went to see for themselves. They took a trail for ox carts some way from the river, until they approached a wooded area near Svay Chrum hospital, no more than eight kilometres from Phum Andong. Silently they crept through a grove of mango trees at the side of the hospital, knowing that they risked their lives. Discovery would mean certain execution. They hid some distance from the hospital, and waited until the boat pulled in to disembark its passengers. Upon landing the men were separated from the women and children, and each group was taken to a different building. Only about a dozen soldiers stood guard. The staff of the hospital had been murdered in the purge of Eastern Zone cadres, and the wards emptied of patients. Villagers living in a few houses within earshot of the hospital had been evicted and sent elsewhere.

Bun and his friends were hiding in the trees some distance from the main hospital building. Even though it was dark they did not dare to approach too close in case they were seen. Patients who had died had been buried in shallow graves just beyond where they were hiding, and the smell of death hung in the air. Nearby larger rectangular pits had been dug, and in some half-covered bodies could be seen. Bun was frozen in horror, fear and disbelief as the Khmer Rouge led two or three women and children from the hospital buildings. All were naked: in the hospital they must have been stripped, probably to be searched for valuables. Loudspeakers blared revolutionary songs and music at full volume. A young girl was seized and raped. Others were led to the pits where they were slaughtered like animals by striking the backs of their skulls with hoes or lengths of bamboo. Young children and babies were held by the legs, their heads smashed against palm trees and their broken bodies flung beside their dying mothers in the death pits. Some children were thrown in the air and bayonetted while music drowned their screams.

Men too were led out in twos and threes. They must have seen the bodies in the pits as they left the hospital, and yet they seemed to offer no resistance to their deaths. They walked forward as if mesmerized, and obediently kneeled at the edge of the pit. Their young killers told some to bend forward to make their work easier. Bun could not understand their terrible passivity. Later he tried to rationalize what he had seen. People had lost their minds, in the sense that they no longer retained any capacity to think for themselves. For three years they had obeyed every

Atrocities witnessed by Bun.

order under fear of death. They had worked to the limit of their physical capacities, while mentally they had become blank and mindless. They were no more than automata, responding to the orders of their tormentors. But in reducing men to this state, the Khmer Rouge had destroyed for many their reasons for living — at least for those who had known another life and who could remember the old Kampuchea.

The wretchedly poor illiterate peasant youth who made up the army could be convinced that they were fighting for the Revolution: anything would be better than the poverty they had known. But the Revolution portrayed by the propaganda of the Khmer Rouge left no hope for those who judged the future by another yardstick. The mindless repetition of empty slogans was not enough to convince educated men and women. Even those who had been ready and willing to help the victors build a new, more egalitarian, more just Kampuchea, had become finally disillusioned. By 1978 many "new people" were without hope. Despair had sapped their will to live. They had contracted what the Khmer Rouge called "memory sickness", thinking too much about the past, about life under the previous regime. This debilitating "disease" was born of despair and hopelessness. Its symptoms were that the sufferer no longer cared what happened to him, no longer turned up for work, no longer took any notice of criticism. The only cure was arrest, imprisonment and execution, or slow death by torture and starvation.

Bun realized that men did not try to escape because they were without hope. They did not *want* to live. They were not brave enough to kill themselves, but if someone did the deed for them they would accept their deaths — almost as a gift. Bun's own uncle had been like this. Before boarding the boat he had heard rumours of impending massacre but had gone because, as he had told Bun, he no longer wanted to live. He was a man who had experienced too much tragedy and pain, a man without hope. Bun was convinced his uncle knew he was going to his death because, before he left, he and his wife gave their two children into the care of Bun's grandmother; and yet he had gone readily.

But if the murdered went to their deaths with such terrible resignation, that did not explain the actions of the murderers. Bun could understand how men and women could lose the will to live. He could not understand how men and mere boys could kill in this sickening and horrifying way. Most of the killers were no more than sixteen or seventeen years old, some were even younger. Yet they had killed without compunction, without any sign of moral revulsion, competing with each other in beating in the brains of screaming children. They had laughed and joked together while bayonetting young girls and smashing men's skulls. Were these Kampucheans — Bun's countrymen — whose Buddhist faith had previously so emphasized respect for life? How had these youths been brutalized? How had they been deprived of all moral sensitivity?

The *yothea* were soldiers of the Revolution, recruited from the poorest strata of village youth in the poorest parts of the Southwest. They were proud to be in the army, for this was an honour Angkar conferred only on the most worthy, only those whom it could trust absolutely in the battle to build and defend the new Kampuchea.[4] So they killed for Angkar; they slaughtered all those whose commitment to the nation's construction and defense was, they were told, less than total. In other words, they killed all those potentially weak enough to become traitors, to bow under the struggle and accept the overlordship of their nation's historic enemy, Vietnam. They murdered, these youths, in the service of an ideology which sought to preserve both purity of race and purity of purpose of the Kampuchean Revolution. For years they had been taught, in simple, repetitive terms, to hate their class enemies, the urban bourgeoisie, the "new people", as traitors to the new Kampuchea. These were enemies who had to be destroyed, without pity, as one would kill a lizard or a rat. The *yothea* had been brutalized by frequent exposure to torture and death. When the order came from Angkar to kill, they obeyed.[5]

No contrition was evinced by these killers. The secret of the destination of the death boat was kept so that the people would not panic, not because what was being perpetrated was a crime against humanity. They stole whatever jewellery, watches or gold they could find. They even took clothes and other belongings which later could not help but be recognized. At the place of execution nothing was hidden. The bodies lay in open pits, rotting under the sun and monsoon rain. Some had been carved open and the liver removed to obtain the bile, from which a traditional medicine was made that was supposed to cure fever. Bun believed reports that some soldiers ate human liver in a cannibalistic rite believed to tap the strength and courage of the victim, though he never himself witnessed this.

When Bun and his friends finally tore themselves away from the ghastly scene of massacre, they hardly knew what they were doing. Blindly and fearfully they made their way back to the village, numb and traumatized. The evacuation had begun in Phum Yot and Phum Prek Champa and had moved on to Phum Memol, Phum Kompong Trea and Phum Maesor Prachan. There was only Phum Loeu and Phum Andong to go. Most "new people" from the other hamlets had been taken. Minority people such as Chinese and Chams were preferentially selected, though for the most part only those Chinese who were "new people". Some "new people" with relatives among the "old people" of the village had been spared. But this had not saved Bun's uncle and aunt and no-one knew who might be selected next.

Bun and his companions contacted other young men in Phum Andong. They had to resist. They refused to let themselves be slaughtered like animals. Some had managed to steal knives; one had an axe. Bun had a crude knife. They decided to fight. The best plan would be to attack the Khmer Rouge on the boat. There were too many soldiers in the village and at the hospital. On the boat there were usually no more than five or six young soldiers, usually the youngest, only in their early teens. They could easily be overpowered and killed. It was a desperate venture but they had to try. Even if they succeeded, however, they were undecided what to do. Perhaps attempt to link up with insurgents said to have taken up arms against the regime; perhaps reach Vietnam.

Then, without warning and without explanation, the boat trips stopped. Phum Andong was spared, but not before as many as 1,500 people had been killed from the other six hamlets in Maesor Prachan. More than thirty of Bun's relatives were massacred, including seventeen children, one a baby a few months old. No reason was given for the suspension of the evacuation; but by then the people of Maesor Prachan were in a state of panic and desperation. It had become common knowledge that people were being killed. Some of the Khmer Rouge soldiers had given the jewellery and clothes of their victims to girl friends in the village. There were bloodstains on the clothing worn by some cadres and some soldiers were even said to have boasted that the livers of people from Phnom Penh were delicious.

People were terrified by the killings, but their terror gave them courage. Reports circulated of villages elsewhere turning on soldiers and hacking them to death with machetes and hoes. The young men in Maesor Prachan were ready to do the same. An underground opposition had sprung up, known as the Khmer Blanc (the White Khmer, as opposed to the Khmer Rouge). Spontaneous and disorganized, they claimed to represent no-one although pro-Vietnamese units by this name had fought against Khmer Rouge troops in the early 1970s. The sole motivation for this scattered resistance was a reckless hatred of the Khmer Rouge; their only desire was to kill in revenge as many soldiers and cadres as they could. They claimed to have already killed a number of Khmer Rouge cadres in Peareang district. A few Khmer Blanc came secretly to Maesor Prachan with the offer to help anyone who feared for his life at the hands of the Khmer Rouge. To Bun they seemed very brave, but he did not join them. They had to be constantly on the move. As the oldest son and a husband, Bun had a responsibility to stay and look after his family and Phiny; but he was prepared to fight in the village.

The floods that year were higher than usual, and communication in much of the Eastern Zone was difficult. The Revolutionary Army was unable to move rapidly in pursuit of its opponents, and was forced to curtail its operations. This, together with popular unrest and the activities of the Khmer Blanc and rebel remnants of Eastern Zone units, probably forced the postponement of the regime's "final solution" for the Eastern Zone — massacre of anyone who might conceivably be less than totally committed to the Khmer Rouge (i.e. all "new people"), followed by the forced relocation of as many villages of "old people" as possible. That it was only a postponement was recognized by those who had been spared. But what could be done? Khmer Rouge soldiers were still stationed in the village, arrogantly exercising their authority. Out of fear people continued to obey their every order, for the young cadres still held power over life and death.

But opposition was growing. Dissident Eastern Zone forces were in open rebellion, and in the villages the former tight discipline was breaking down. Restrictions on travel were ignored, at least within Maesor Prachan, for the new hamlet chiefs and committees seemed reluctant to assume the absolute power of those purged earlier in the year. Men and women could mix and converse more freely. The previously strict sexual morality was disregarded, especially by the Khmer Rouge soldiers. Many had girlfriends in the village, either among the new nurses assigned to the village hospital, or the bolder of the village girls from the mobile brigade. The soldiers' girls were much feared in Maesor Prachan for the power they could wield. Especially hated was a swarthy girl called Sy Kim. If someone insulted her, she would point out the culprit to her boy friend, Husot, and that person would later disappear. A murder more or less meant little to men who had killed so many. some of the soldiers flaunted the watches of their victims. When they patrolled the village on motorbikes, their appearance was enough to strike fear.

But opposition was growing in other ways. Probably the most unpopular aspect of life was communal dining. Many people went to the kitchens to demand their utensils back, and began eating at home. When district cadres became aware of what was happening they called a meeting of all the people to order a return to communal eating. To enforce their demand, they said that until everyone complied, no salt would be sent to the village or distributed. In the hot and humid climate of Kampuchea, lack of salt for a period of ten to fifteen days was enough to make people weak and dizzy, but this use of salt as a weapon to divide and intimidate people only had the effect of strengthening their determination to resist Khmer Rouge dictates. Some of the cooks had already hidden supplies of salt, which could also be obtained secretly on the black market which had grown up. A kilogram of salt sold for one *damleung* of gold. The Khmer Rouge cadres tried to stop this trade by enforcing the prohibition against movement outside the village. A night curfew was introduced. But by this time "old" and "new people" were united against the regime. All cooperated to subvert the new regulations and no-one reported those who broke the curfew. As the soldiers all came from the Southwest they did not know the people of Maesor Prachan. The dogs barked at them, so it was impossible for them to patrol quietly at night. An order to kill all the dogs in the village was disregarded, though the soldiers killed many themselves.

Both "old" and "new" people formed a village guard together, to monitor the movements of army patrols. The soldiers were by then quite isolated from the people, a military garrison totally out of touch with those they were there to control. Bun was a member of the guard in Phum Andong. Armed with his knife, he was assigned duty on a regular roster with other men in the hamlet. One of his duties was to stand guard when people in the village tried to pick up Khmer broadcasts by Voice of America or the radio of the Kampuchea National United Front for National Salvation (KNUFNS) set up by Khmer dissidents with Vietnamese support and with headquarters in Vietnam's Tay Ninh province. The radio receiver had previously been well hidden; now it was set up openly in the dining hall, powered by car batteries and a pedal-driven dynamo — an indication of the extent to which people were by then prepared to act in defiance of the Khmer Rouge.

With the coming of the dry season, a new unit of Khmer Rouge troops moved into the village. Several times Khmer Blanc guerrillas slipped into Maesor Prachan to urge the people to rebel against the regime. They were listened to with respect.

Khmer Rouge authority begins to be flouted.

Some men went underground and joined the Khmer Blanc resistance. No-one trusted the Khmer Rouge. Everyone believed it was only a matter of time before mass killings began again. Rumour had it that the great pit excavated to provide fill for the Tonle Toch dam was to be used for the mass burial of the entire village. This was not as preposterous as it sounded, since the Khmer Rouge were known to be fanatical in their determination to purge the whole of the Eastern Zone.

When the high water receded and the mass re-location of villages began, the people of Maesor Prachan were convinced this was a pretext for another massacre. But the Khmer Rouge came to the village in force. They explained that everyone had to move northwest into the forests of Kompong Cham province where they would re-establish the village. This was necessary, they said, because situated where it was the village was vulnerable to infiltration by enemy spies and traitors who were plotting the overthrow of Democratic Kampuchea. People were ordered to take with them only what they could carry. They were to go on foot, guarded from Khmer Blanc attack by Khmer Rouge troops.

As before, the move began with the hamlets furthest from Phum Andong. In December 1978 the people of Phum Yot, Phum Memol and Phum Prek Champa were ordered to move out. Some who tried to escape were summarily executed. Though most people were convinced they would be killed, they had no alternative but to go. Even the Khmer Blanc resistance was powerless to prevent the evacuation. The people of Phum Andong discussed what could be done. Despite the executions, some still hoped to escape. But time was running out.

Then, without warning on 25 December 1978, before the relocation of Maesor Prachan could proceed further, the armed forces of the Socialist Republic of Vietnam launched a massive offensive against their communist neighbour. The Vietnamese invasion was nominally in support of forces of the KNUFNS under the leadership of a former Khmer Rouge brigade commander named Heng Samrin. By 2 January 1979, the Kampuchean army was in full retreat. The Vietnamese entered Phnom Penh on 7 January, while Pol Pot and the remainder of his forces withdrew to prearranged jungle bases to carry on a protracted war against the occupying forces. Once again, by what divine force or stroke of fortune he did not know, Bun and his family had been saved from almost certain death.

For others release from Khmer Rouge domination did not come until later. Savath Pou, former high-school teacher and assistant headmaster of Svay Rieng high school, and his family were transported in September 1978 from Krachap village, six kilometres from the Vietnamese border in Prey Veng province, to the village of Kamreng in Maung district of Battambang province. The move, by boat, train, and foot, took two weeks, and initially involved only thirteen families, including three families of "old people" accused of having "Vietnamese minds in Khmer bodies". It seems to have been ordered to prevent any concerted move on the part of the villagers to flee to Vietnam to join the KNUFNS, as many were then doing.

At Kamreng the family found itself one of a hundred or so "new" families outnumbering the ten or fifteen families of original inhabitants left. No reason had been given for the move from Krachap, except that the government had decided to transport people to Battambang because it was the richest rice growing province. Nothing was said about an imminent Vietnamese attack. But at Kamreng food supplies were even more meagre than at Krachap. Even after the Vietnamese invaded, villagers knew nothing of the event; the struggle for food consumed all their energies. Savath delivered his last child himself after the rural midwife refused to attend a "new" family. He was forced to feed his three children on boiled bark and roots to keep them alive. Many children died when a measles epidemic broke out. In their weakened state few had the stamina to fight off the disease, but Savath's children survived.

In Kamreng everyone lived in terror. Although there were only between seven and ten Khmer Rouge cadres in the village, no-one thought of attacking them or escaping. This despite the fact that the "new people" knew they had been sent to the village suspected of being pro-Vietnamese, and believed that eventually they would all be killed. But there were Khmer Rouge troops stationed in the vicinity, and revolt would have been mercilessly punished.

Every few nights the cadres came to arrest a man, tie his hands, and take him to the forest to be killed. Sometimes he would be forced to dig a shallow grave: often the head was cut off with a large machete and the body left lying where it fell, to be discovered later by the villagers. No reason was given for any execution, though the Khmer Rouge made it known that those who did not work as hard as they could thereby demonstrated their lukewarm commitment to the regime. But this was no more than a ploy to prevent panic, and to mask the systematic nature of the killing. Every "new" family was marked for death. usually the father would be taken first, either at night or while working.

Sometimes women and children would be killed a few days later; sometimes they would be spared. No-one knew why. Savath lived in constant fear from night to night; every sound terrified him. He never knew when it would be his turn to be killed. All he could do was to work his hardest, and hope that others would be taken first.

As Vietnamese forces fanned out through the country, encountering pockets of Khmer Rouge resistance, the rate of killing was stepped up in Kamreng village. Not until May 1979 did Heng Samrin's forces reach Maung district. The Khmer Rouge fled to the Cardamom ranges, taking with them perhaps a third of the population of the district. Many families, both "old" and "new", went willingly for fear of the Vietnamese. Others tried to escape in the commotion. In Kamreng village about 100 cadres and soldiers tried to shepherd thousands of people towards the mountains. Savath Pou delayed his departure for as long as he could and was lucky enough to make contact with a contingent of Heng Samrin's troops. In escaping with them he and his family came under fire from the Khmer Rouge, but were unharmed. After months of constant fear, the nightmare was over.

Almost everywhere Heng Samrin's troops and the Vietnamese were welcomed as liberators. In many areas the people themselves turned on the Khmer Rouge. From the end of December, broken and beaten groups of fleeing Revolutionary Army troops passed through Maesor Prachan. At the time three Khmer Blanc guerrillas, armed with Chinese AK-47 automatic rifles, were hiding in the village and with the help of the locals, they set up an ambush. A group of seven exhausted and hungry Khmer Rouge troops, heavily armed with automatic weapons and bazookas, were invited to a meal in the communal dining hall in Phum Loeu. For days the young soldiers had not slept as they retreated before the advancing Vietnamese. When the seven left the dining hall, the Khmer Blanc opened fire on them from concealed positions and more than a hundred villagers, armed only with axes and knives, rushed in to finish them off. The Khmer Rouge were able to return some of the fire, including a bazooka round at point blank range, but miraculously none of the attackers was hit. Those soldiers still alive were hacked to death, their bodies savagely mutilated in a spontaneous rage for revenge.

Twice more the same pattern of events was repeated, and the captured weapons distributed to villagers. Bun took part in one ambush but was not given a weapon. Later he and others were almost caught in crossfire apparently between rival Khmer

Rouge units fighting each other as they retreated. Such acts of revenge against Kampuchean soldiers were repeated in many villages in the Eastern Zone during the Vietnamese advance. But Khmer Rouge troops were killed not to assist the Vietnamese — few Khmer then had much love for them — but purely as revenge for the pain and terror and misery of the previous years. No action could have demonstrated more clearly the total loss of popular support for Angkar that had occurred. Once the purges of June had weakened the iron hold the Party had over a cowed and demoralized rural population, people began, in regaining a measure of control over their own lives, to regain some courage and initiative. The massacres in July brought "old" and "new" people together in revulsion and horror, and destroyed the last remaining loyalties all but a fanatical few had for the regime. Angkar, in the form of an occupying army of teenage sadists foreign to the region, lost its last shreds of respect and authority — just as the government of Lon Nol, corrupt and discredited, had done less than four years before.

CHAPTER 9

Democratic Kampuchea

Any attempt to understand what happened in Kampuchea during those terrible years from 1975 to 1979 must dig deeply into both Kampuchean history and the Khmer mind.[1] The perception Kampucheans have of their own past forms an essential part of the Khmer world view. In particular it shapes the attitudes Kampucheans have towards their neighbours, especially the Vietnamese. The image they have of themselves is also in part a reflection of these attitudes. In the warped view of the world which developed and festered in the minds of the handful of men and women around Pol Pot at the summit of power in the Communist Party of Kampuchea, the relation between history and race was crucial in their assessment both of the dangers they believed faced the Kampuchean state, and of the historic task which they believed they were called upon to accomplish. Both their own revolutionary experience, and the opposition which developed to their policies, only served to confirm them in their convictions, especially as the quickening pace of events seemed increasingly to create conditions leading to the fulfilment of their worst fears — invasion by Vietnam, destruction of the Kampuchean state, and the threat of the eventual elimination of the Khmer race.

An important underlying element in the Khmer Rouge world view was the threat of national extinction. Every educated

Khmer Blanc and villagers take revenge.

Khmer, communist and non-communist alike, gloried in the greatness of the ancient Khmer empire with its capital at Angkor, near Siem Reap. All knew that most of the Mekong delta of southern Vietnam, southern Laos, and much of northeast and central Thailand once formed part of the Khmer state. But as the power of Angkor declined, these areas were lost — to the Thai extending their control over the rice plains of the lower Menam, to the Lao on both banks of the Mekong, and to the Vietnamese in their "march to the south". It was the Thai who finally sacked Angkor and forced a relocation of the Khmer capital to the vicinity of Phnom Penh; but the Vietnamese were most feared. The Thai disputed territory with the Khmer, but the two races had much in common, notably cultural similarities deriving from their common religion, Theravada Buddhism. In their thrust south the Vietnamese destroyed the kingdom of Champa previously incorporating all of what is now central Vietnam, and virtually annihilated the Cham race. A few Cham fled to Kampuchea, a few remained in Vietnam, but in both places they were reduced to little more than a depressed minority. Of the great state whose navies sailed up the Mekong to battle the Khmer on the lake of Tonle Sap, nothing remained.[2]

The fate of the Chams cannot have been far from the minds of Kampuchean leaders when, in the 1830s, the Vietnamese Emperor Minh Mang attempted to extend Vietnamese control over the Khmer state. Most of Kampuchea was occupied by Vietnamese forces. Vietnamese mandarins enforced a policy of wholesale Vietnamization. Theravada Buddhism, as the principal vehicle of Kampuchean culture, was actively persecuted. Vietnamese cultural values were forcibly imposed, including the wearing of Vietnamese garments. Even place names were changed. Such a thorough-going programme of cultural imperialism met with Kampuchean resistance, and ended in popular revolt. With Thai help the Vietnamese were driven out, but Kampuchean independence remained tenuous.

The French protectorate established over Kampuchea in 1863 ended a period of joint Thai and Vietnamese hegemony over the Khmer monarchy. Thereafter Thai influence waned. But during the colonial period France ruled her Indochinese empire from Vietnam and Vietnamese interests were consistently placed ahead of those of Kampuchea. While Kampucheans resented these developments, most Vietnamese saw them as perfectly natural — so much so that Vietnamese revolutionaries took it for granted that their revolution should take precedence over anything happening in Kampuchea. Insurgency in Kampuchea, whether against the French, Sihanouk, or Lon Nol, was useful in Vietnamese eyes primarily for the support it gave to their own struggle, first against the French and then against the Americans.

For the ardent young Khmer Marxist intellectuals returning from their studies in France during the 1950s and 1960s this Vietnamese attitude, which they both sensed and which was spelled out to them, was intolerable. Yet the logic of the Vietnamese position had considerable force. Once the Americans were expelled from Vietnam, Sihanouk would no longer be of value. With Vietnamese support, his regime would fall like a rotten fruit. But the Khmer revolutionaries were impatient for action. If they failed to mount their own revolution and win their own victory, and waited instead for Vietnamese assistance, would they not be so beholden to the Vietnamese that they would no longer be masters in their own country? Wouldn't Hanoi's influence over the Kampuchean Revolution be so great that the Vietnamese would be in a position to shape it to their own interests? Such a possibility had already been foreshadowed in the concept of an Indochinese Federation to include Vietnam, Kampuchea, and Laos. Unquestionably Vietnam would be the senior partner, a situation which would pose a standing threat to the independence, and even the national sovereignty and territorial integrity of Kampuchea.[3]

The first two decades of Kampuchean independence from France was a period of intense nationalism. Much of Sihanouk's political success at this time came from his ability to mobilize nationalist sentiments, especially through his prickly insistence on Kampuchean independence and neutrality in the face of encroachments on Kampuchean territory by the Republic of Vietnam or United States forces. At first anti-Vietnamese feelings were focussed against the government of South Vietnam; but as an American withdrawal became increasingly likely, more and more Kampucheans saw the principal threat as coming from a unified, powerful, Vietnamese communist regime — a regime which already was disregarding the sovereignty of Kampuchea by occupying not inconsiderable areas of the country (even if by agreement with Sihanouk).

Leftist insurgents were as influenced by the resurgence of Khmer nationalism as was the political right. They were equally concerned about long-term Vietnamese intentions, and equally determined not to submit to Vietnamese hegemony. For Kampuchean Marxists "proletarian internationalism" was unacceptable if this meant that Vietnamese interests should come first.

And yet, of course, they remained dependent on Hanoi. Even when Sihanouk was deposed, and there was no longer any reason for North Vietnam to restrain the Khmer Rouge, the CPK was still dependent on the Vietnam People's Army to counter cross-border invasions from South Vietnam. It was a dependency which rankled, but one which the CPK decision not to follow Hanoi's example and negotiate with the US abruptly terminated — at least as far as the Khmer revolutionaries were concerned. The eradication of Vietnamese influence in the CPK through the murder of almost all cadres who had returned from North Vietnam symbolized this termination of Kampuchean dependency in a brutal and forceful way. It was an expression too of the depth of distrust which had already developed in the CPK of Vietnamese communist intentions.

The Khmer Rouge victory of April 1975 had an exhilarating but distorting effect on thinking within the Party. Phnom Penh had fallen two weeks before Saigon. The Khmer Revolution had been victorious before the Vietnamese. Under the leadership of the CPK it had triumphed against all odds; and it owed nothing to the Vietnamese. Or so it was believed. The decision to refuse to negotiate and to fight on alone, despite horrendous losses, had therefore been the right one. It seemed to the Khmer Rouge in their exultation that the Kampuchean Revolution had triumphed through its own strength alone; through, above all, the absolute discipline and dedication of its cadres and troops. Its very success stood as witness to Khmer invincibility. Backed by the socialist revolution conducted by the CPK in the Kampuchean countryside, the Party had transformed the Kampuchean peasantry through strict discipline and unquestioning commitment from an exploited, passive mass to an indomitable force that had, so the Khmer Rouge proclaimed, not simply overthrown a corrupt and unpopular dictatorship, but also defeated the most powerful imperialist state of all, the United States of America.

No mention was ever made in Democratic Kampuchea of Vietnamese support during the liberation struggle. Yet as Sihanouk himself has pointed out, it was VPA main force troops who bore the brunt of fighting against invading American and South Vietnamese forces in 1970. To deny this, as Sihanouk stated in his *Chroniques de guerre . . . et d'espoir*, is not only to insult former allies, but is "an insult to history"; and "history" will admit neither bad faith nor lies".[4] More to the point, such distortion of fact led only to self-deception, to the belief that an army of "poor and lower-middle peasants" was invincible, and could achieve unparalleled feats in both peace and war — providing their solidarity, their pure, hard resolution was not undermined and sabotaged by those whose commitment to the Revolution was less than absolute. Thus the experience of a leadership whose success in war had surprised even themselves was transferred to the quite different requirements of administering a nation at peace. The military discipline of war was applied in a society at peace, in the conviction that only a population so disciplined and dedicated could build and defend the new Kampuchean state.[5]

More sinister for the Khmer people, or at least for a large proportion of them, was that the Khmer Rouge could argue that their victory had been achieved with no help at all from more than half the population — all those who remained in the cities, unheeding of the call to join the revolutionary forces. For the Khmer Rouge, these were people who had failed to recognize the Revolution for what it was — the greatest event in Kampuchean history. But how could they have failed to see its historic necessity when illiterate peasants flocked to its banner? Because, in the eyes of the radical nationalist members of the CPK grouped around Pol Pot, such people had lost their intuitive identity with the Khmer soul; they were no longer truly Khmer. People in the cities, even those who did not fight or work for Lon Nol, had been so influenced by imperialist and capitalist culture that they had lost contact with their own cultural heritage. Since they had opposed the Revolution, if only through inaction, they could not be trusted to dedicate themselves to the building of a new Kampuchea, or to oppose the nation's enemies. If they were inactive during the Revolution, would they not also remain inactive in the face of Vietnamese attempts to subvert the Kampuchean state and enslave the Khmer people? And would not their weakness weaken the resolution of others? The logical conclusion of such reasoning was that if the Revolution were under threat such people would have to be eliminated, if only to preserve in the remainder of the population that absolute revolutionary fervour which alone would again prove invincible against all enemies, as it had during the years from 1970 to 1975.

Such are the implications of the failure of the Khmer Rouge to analyze realistically the nature of their own revolution. Equally unrealistic was their economic thinking, influenced as it was by the radical Maoism of the Great Leap Forward and the Cultural Revolution. The radical nationalists were determined to build in the shortest possible time a new Kampuchea capable of withstanding whatever pressure Vietnam might bring to bear. The economic measures the leadership thought necessary to achieve this aim had been foreshadowed years earlier in the theses produced in Paris by Khieu Samphan and Hou Youn. Hou Youn had argued that towns and cities, far from contributing to the production of wealth in a country like Kampuchea with a predominantly agricultural economy, merely drained the wealth of the rural areas, leaving the peasantry in a state of misery, barely surviving on a fraction of their just and proper earnings. "The trees grow in the rural areas, but the fruit goes to the towns", he wrote.

More influential in Khmer Rouge thinking was the thesis of Khieu Samphan, who argued that the backwardness of the Kampuchean economy was essentially due to its integration into an international economic order dominated by advanced capitalist states. If Kampuchea with its own underdeveloped dual economic structure (a precapitalist agricultural sector in the countryside and an atrophied capitalist sector in the towns) wanted to develop and industrialize, Khieu Samphan argued, it had to wrench itself free of this international integration, and pursue instead an autonomous development policy. The state alone had the power to do this by taking over the role of commercial middleman in exporting surplus agricultural production and directing investment in industry — but only after Kampuchea's existing "semi-colonial and semi-feudal" socio economic structure had been destroyed. Such arguments led naturally to the Khmer Rouge policy of economic autarchy.[6]

In evacuating the towns and abolishing markets and money the Khmer Rouge acted in the belief that the urban commercial middle class was parasitic and produced no real wealth. Only factory workers should live in towns, merchants were better engaged in agricultural production, to increase the surplus rice, rubber and other primary products marketed by the state to provide capital for industrial investment. Export earnings would no longer be siphoned off to be frittered away on luxury imports, since no-one would any longer be accumulating the private wealth to purchase them. The whole nation would be made up of industrial workers and subsistence peasant farmers, together comprising a single class, hardened by physical labour, unified in militant solidarity and committed to Angkar and the Kampuchean Revolution. Such a policy, it was believed, would create a nation of Khmer similar to those "pure and hard" peasants whose revoutionary heroism had been victorious in the struggle against U.S. imperialism. Such a nation could alone withstand the Vietnamese.

But vigilance was constantly needed. Even though American

Khieu Samphan

Ieng Sary

imperialism had been defeated, the insidious nature of capitalism could still undermine the unity, solidarity and national commitment of the Khmer people to the socialist construction and defense of their country. No decadent cultural influences could be permitted to find their way into Kampuchea from the West — nothing, not even trade, that might conceivably open the way for capitalist penetration of the Kampuchean economy. Only Chinese technical assistance was acceptable. Kampuchea would never again be drawn into an international system in which it could not hope to be other than a weak and dependent member. Its independence and sovereignty, upon which national survival so vitally depended, would be hopelessly compromised, and the new, hard, pure socialist Kampuchea would be destroyed.

In order to prevent this happening the Khmer people had to be completely unified and totally dedicated. All waverers had to be weeded out. Even a quarter of the population, a mere two million soldiers and farmers, would be sufficient to recreate Khmer greatness if they drew their strength from their purity of race and the soil of Kampuchea. Even two million Khmer, at a ratio of one to thirty, could still triumph over sixty million Vietnamese. But they had to be pure Kampucheans, undiluted by alien minorities (Chinese, Cham, hill tribes), and untouched by alien culture. Anyone married to a foreigner, any child of mixed descent, any Khmer educated abroad, anyone arguing a more moderate line — all represented potential weakness, which had to be eliminated.

The same kind of reasoning was also applied to the Party. All opposition to Centre policies was believed to be either due to Vietnamese conspiracies, or designed to assist Vietnam by weakening the Khmer state. Traitors had therefore to be rooted out. Above all, the Party, as guardian and director of the Kampuchean Revolution, had to be united in its will to resist Vietnamese treachery. If the nation was to be strengthened and retain its independence, the Party had to be entirely composed of the purest of the pure. No matter what the cost, the Party had to be purged of any weak member: every debilitating influence had to be rooted out and eliminated, and every means to this end could legitimately be employed — indeed, had to be employed. Factionalism in the Party had to be overcome, for any internal divisions could be exploited by the Vietnamese in order to destroy the Khmer Revolution and impose Hanoi's political will on Kampuchea.

Fear and hatred of Vietnam as the greatest threat to national survival, Khmer racism, economic autarchy, and an obsession with the need for absolute political power and Party unity — all these were ingredients in the radical nationalist world view. Pol Pot and his cohorts believed that the Kampuchean nation, poor and weak, had to be strengthened and steeled. There was no time to lose: none knew how soon Vietnam would strike. What had happened in Laos was taken was a warning. There the Vietnamese exercised decisive political influence. The 1977 Treaty of Friendship and Cooperation between Laos and Vietnam convinced the Khmer Rouge that Laos had been locked into a *de facto* Vietnamese-dominated "federation". They believed that if the Vietnamese had their way, they would impose a similar relationship on Kampuchea. It was necessary to resist this by strengthening the Khmer state while simultaneously holding the Vietnamese at bay, and by amassing as great an agricultural surplus as possible in the shortest possible time while making military forays across the border with Vietnam in order to keep the Vietnamese off-balance.

Radical nationalist thinking can be seen to have had its own twisted logic, but the contradictions inherent in the application of Centre policies instead of generating Party unity only increased opposition among those in the Party who could see where they were leading. A policy of massive accumulation accompanying increased production levels would only have been acceptable to the Kampuchean people if living standards had improved and food consumption increased. But the reverse was happening, and the consequent popular discontent was evident to any cadre in contact with the people, whether "new" or "old". Still, that discontent might have been contained had the need for it been better explained; and as a policy of necessity it might have drawn more support within the CPK had the surplus been channelled to more productive ends. But given the escalating conflict with Vietnam, too much was going to pay for armaments and feed the armed forces. Those in the Party who opposed the Pol Pot faction argued both that more concern should be shown for people, and that more conciliatory policies should be adopted towards Vietnam. But the radical nationalists feared that any concessions would weaken their own hold on the Party, thereby leading to the accession to power of pro-Vietnamese elements who would compromise Kampuchean independence.

All opposition was therefore seen as traitorous, part of a Vietnamese plot to overthrow the radical nationalist leadership of the CPK, to dispose of the only group who could defeat Vietnamese designs to establish political control over Kampuchea. As a result, criticism was never evaluated and taken into consideration: it was simply labelled as treason and dealt with accordingly. The cycle of repression, conflict with Vietnam, and purge continued unbroken. By the time it became clear that the Vietnamese were actively organizing and arming opponents of the Khmer Rouge regime, it was too late for the radical nationalists even to admit their mistakes, let alone change their policies. The Vietnamese action merely confirmed their conviction that Hanoi had been behind every dissident voice in the CPK, and convinced them of the need to continue the purges. Once all opposition had been eliminated inside Kampuchea, the Vietnamese could only gain support from the few Kampuchean refugees in Vietnam — and these would pose no threat to the regime, provided China continued to lend Kampuchea its support. The role of the Chinese in events in Kampuchea from 1975 to 1978 should not be overestimated. The radical nationalists looked to China to support Kampuchea against Vietnam: in fact some of the continuing hostility towards Vietnam may have been designed to ensure Chinese military assistance. But the Chinese made it clear to the Kampucheans that they were on their own: any Vietnamese invasion would have to be met by guerrilla war. Part of the economy had therefore to be directed to this end. Even as more rice and other agricultural products were exported to China in exchange for arms, throughout 1978 additional food supplies were stockpiled in mountainous areas which could serve as bases for guerrilla resistance.

Yet some, even at this late hour, reacted against fatalistic acceptance of an invasion which could only result in the overthrow of the regime. Among those who apparently called for a change of direction was a long-time supporter of the radical nationalist faction, Deputy Prime Minister in charge of the Economy, Vorn Veth. According to Ieng Sary, he committed suicide after an unsuccessful attempted coup against the Party Centre in November 1978. With him were purged two other ministers in the government, Cheng An (Industry) and Mey Prang (Communications).

The cycle of purges, of which those of November 1978 were the last, was the means by which the Pol Pot faction attempted to consolidate its own dictatorship. The purges themselves reveal much about the thinking of the radical nationalist leadership. Pol Pot and his cohorts converted the CPK into a Stalinist party, an organization of men and women loyal to the Party leader and prepared, without question, to carry out the policies of the Party

Centre.[7] They thus saw opposition within the Party in the same light, as a rival network of personal loyalties which had to be rooted out. And because all such opposition was believed to be Vietnamese-inspired, it was, in large part and as indicated above, the logic of paranoia over Vietnamese intentions towards Kampuchea which, together with the megalomania of absolute dictatorship, led directly to the terror and insanity of Tuol Sleng.

Tuol Sleng stands as a lasting symbol of the crass brutality of the Khmer Rouge regime.[8] The prison comprised four large three-storey concrete buildings with a separate single-story office block where the prison archives were housed. One block was reserved for women, and classrooms in another had been converted into small brick cells for the solitary confinement of more important prisoners. Other prisoners were crammed together, dozens to a room. Records that remain show that 154 prisoners were admitted in 1975; 2,250 in 1976; 6,330 in 1977; and 5,765 for the first six months of 1978. After that records are lost. The recorded total of 14,449 prisoners should therefore probably be increased to at least 18,000 — a figure which does not include as many as 2,000 children estimated to have been kept at the prison with their parents but not included in the records. Of these 20,000, a mere handful remain alive.

During 1977 and 1978 between 1,000 and 1,500 prisoners were usually being held at any one time in Tuol Sleng. For example, on 20 April 1978 there were 1,242 prisoners, 105 of them women. They were categorized according to army unit, region or government ministry. On that date, for example, fifty-seven army officers were being held, sixty-eight from the Interior Ministry, and forty-eight from the Ministry of Industry, and so on. Of the different zones, 436 were held from the Eastern Zone reflecting the severity of the purge there leading up to the fall of So Phim, while only five were from the Central Zone and forty from the Southwest. Prisoners were usually executed in batches when numbers built up too high, and were buried in mass graves. The most recorded killed on any one day was 582 on 27 May 1978, almost all of them soldiers from the Eastern Zone Army who had, as commanded, surrendered their arms to Central Army forces during the Eastern Zone purges. Mass killings also took place during October 1977.

Most of those tortured and killed at Tuol Sleng were Khmer Rouge cadres (and their wives and children). But more than a thousand other victims have been recorded. These include a surprising 324 factory workers; 206 former Lon Nol army officers; 113 teachers and University professors; 87 foreigners, mainly

Lao and Thai, but including a few Vietnamese, Indians and Caucasians; 148 Khmer intellectuals and technicians who returned from abroad of their own free will to serve the new regime, and who were arrested on their return as spies; and 194 students, many of whom must have demonstrated against the Lon Nol government on behalf of the Khmer Rouge in the spring of 1975.

Interrogation took place in a separate building across the road from the prison until 1978, when the women's block was taken over for this purpose. Minute records were kept of everything admitted by victims under torture, including particularly the names of anyone else inculpated. These were then cross-referenced against other confessions, and complicated flow-charts of presumed traitorous contacts were drawn up. Those whose names figured on such lists would be arrested, providing their whereabouts were known. As most of those mentioned by party cadres were other members of the party with whom the victim had fought during the revolution, or worked since 1975, this process was most destructive of the CPK itself. Torture was systematic, its use noted as a matter of course in reports on important prisoners. The aim of such torture was to reduce the victim to a state of total psychological acquiescence, so that he or she would cooperate in a process of self-incrimination. Prisoners were chained to beds, starved, beaten, and pierced with steel skewers; they were degraded, humiliated, disorientated. When Vietnamese troops entered the prison on 7 January 1979, guards had fled, but the bodies of fourteen torture victims were still manacled to their beds. Blood, hair and faeces spattered the walls.

The more than 10,000 dossiers of charges and confessions that make up the prison records of Tuol Sleng provide an horrific insight into the twisted, lunatic world of Democratic Kampuchea's leaders. This vast store of material will take years for historians to examine, and a scholarly study of the Khmer Rouge State Security apparatus is yet to be written. One dossier which has been examined is that of Hu Nim, former Minister of Information and Propaganda in the government of Democratic Kampuchea, and former comrade-in-arms of Pol Pot and Ieng Sary. The dossier consists of over 200 pages of confessions, dating from the time of his arrest (10 April 1977) to his execution almost three months later (6 July 1977). Hu Nim was a former journalist with a French doctorate in law. Loquacious and opinionated, he was nevertheless respected for his polemical abilities. He was deeply influenced by the Chinese Cultural

Revolution, and his political beliefs have been characterized as "a kind of nationalist Maoism". From his series of confessions it is possible to piece together not only the supposed crimes which justified his execution, but also the basis of his political opposition to the ruling radical nationalist clique that was the real reason he was killed.

The burden of Hu Nim's final confession is that he had long and secretly been "an officer of the CIA, serving the activities of the CIA, serving American imperialism and opposing communism ... and successfully heading towards the construction of capitalism in Kampuchea, completely toeing the line of the Free World and the American imperialists". The transparent absurdity of this admission by one who had, in the course of a life-long dedication to the cause of socialist revolution, spent years fighting in the jungle, leaves one dumbfounded. His political opposition to the radical nationalists has to be gleaned from a comment here, an aside there. Against the political line of radical autarchy, Hu Nim seems to have believed that some appropriate technology could be borrowed from capitalist countries — tractors, for example, and perhaps some agricultural machinery such as irrigation pumps. Hu Nim was "disturbed and tormented" by the Party policy of collectivism, especially the compulsory communal dining which proved so unpopular; and he was concerned over the severity of administrative and political purges. According to a Khmer Rouge defector interviewed in Thailand after the Vietnamese invasion, Hu Nim had argued that "working people must not be persecuted, and foreign aid must be accepted so that the Kampuchean people do not suffer too much". Thus the core of his opposition to the Pol Pot faction appears to have been that in pursuit of their policies they were pushing the Kampuchean people beyond the limits of their endurance. The burden was too great; repression too harsh; the means of subsistence available to them too slender.

For the radical nationalists to accept such an argument was impossible, however, for in their fanatical logic it would lead not only to their own demise, but also in all probability to the extinction of the Khmer people and the Kampuchean state. To admit they had been wrong would be to open the way for their enemies, those who would compromise with Vietnam, so there could be no turning back. Only the radical nationalists could guide the Khmer people in construction of their own form of socialism and defence of their own Revolution. They alone had the vision necessary to create a people hardened by the purifying virtue of physical labour, invigorated through struggle, unsullied by any foreign influence, and united in will to resist the hated enemy, Vietnam.

How could such a glorious goal not fire the hearts of all true Kampuchean patriots? Any opponents could only be men who had succumbed to the insidious lure of Western imperialism, or who had sold out to the Vietnamese, men who placed their personal comfort or ambition before the national good. Those arguing, like Hu Nim, for an end to autarchy would open the floodgates of Western influence; those calling for a more moderate policy towards the masses might weaken them to the point where they could no longer withstand the Vietnamese. Such men also destroyed the essential unity of the nation by sapping the solidarity and dedication of the Party. They represented a weakness in the struggle for national survival. For the sake of the nation and the Party, they had to be weeded out. But they should not be simply killed, for there was one last valuable service they could render to the Revolution: they could provide information about the thinking of their comrades; they could reveal other traitors in the Party and its organs.

So Hu Nim and those who thought like him, and had had the courage to speak out within the Party, were tortured, confessed all, and were executed. Former student leader Phouk Chhay was killed the same day, and Hu Nim's wife was executed too. The Party had triumphed, for the Party was just. Angkar was ever victorious — but at a fearful price. Not only did the terrible logic of the radical nationalist faction lead to the decimation of the CPK, it also led through reliance on ever younger, ever more ignorant and brutal cadres, to the loss of all popular support for the regime. Where the only punishment is death, all respect for those in power is destroyed, for they are seen as killers.

Blood in Kampuchea became under the Khmer Rouge a symbol and an obsession. Blood held a fascination. The words of the national anthem proclaim in official translation:

Bright red Blood which covers towns and plains
Of Kampuchea, our Motherland,
Sublime Blood of workers and peasants,
Sublime Blood of revolutionary men and women fighters!

The Blood changing into unrelenting hatred
And resolute struggle
On April 17th, under the Flag of the Revolution,
Frees from slavery!

The blood of the Khmer Rouge did seem to have been changed into unrelenting hatred. But the blood that continued to be spilled as a result of that hatred, a hatred increasingly directed against their own people, symbolized for most Kampucheans not freedom, but enslavement. Only blood spilled kept the regime in power: only in blood could such a regime be overthrown.

CHAPTER 10

The Coming
of the Vietnamese

The timely arrival of the Vietnamese was welcomed in the Eastern Zone, and indeed throughout Kampuchea.[1] It was evident from the beginning that the Vietnamese were well prepared for the invasion, and that they intended to remain in occupation of the country. Vietnamese soldiers at first wore the uniforms of the forces of the Kampuchean National United Front for National Salvation. They flew the flag of the Front (the former flag of the Khmer Issarak), very similar to that of the Khmer Rouge except that the outline of the temple of Angkor Wat in the centre had five instead of three towers. Bun was impressed by the way Vietnamese troops seemed to go out of their way to be polite and considerate to the Kampucheans they encountered. They spoke of themselves as liberating the Khmer people from the terrible yoke of the Khmer Rouge.

Not until 8 January 1979 did the first Vietnamese troops pass through Maesor Prachan and occupy the district capital of Snaypol. There they announced the abolition of communal dining, the re-opening of markets, freedom to practise religion and refurbish pagodas, and freedom of individual movement. Festivities to celebrate the overthrow of the Khmer Rouge were quickly organized at which traditional dances and songs were performed for the first time in almost four years. Vietnamese troops joined in the celebrations, mingled with the Khmer

The Vietnamese received as liberators.

Festivities to celebrate the overthrow of Khmer Rouge.

crowds, and took part in the dances. In the immediate relief that the sufferings of the past were at an end, these changes met with universal acclaim. Considering the relentlessness of anti-Vietnamese propaganda under the Khmer Rouge, and that almost every Kampuchean had learned to see Vietnam as the nation's historic enemy, the warmth with which Vietnamese forces were welcomed came as something of a surprise, even to the Vietnamese. But it was a product of circumstances, rather than a national change of heart; it rested not on any real affection for historic enemies, but on the depth of hatred felt for the Khmer Rouge. So long as the memory of those terrible years remained, so long as there was even the remotest possibility that Pol Pot and his minions might reimpose their rule on Kampuchea, the Vietnamese would be welcome. Longer than that and they would not be seen as liberators, but would become an occupying army.

In Maesor Prachan the changes were welcome. People who had survived the move to Kampong Cham province from the hamlets of Phum Yot, Phum Memol and Phum Prek Champa began to return home. Each family was henceforth responsible for its own affairs. By common agreement rice was distributed to each family according to the number of members, and vegetable gardens and fruit trees once again became private property. But in reaction to the sudden change of regime people seemed disorientated. They were happy, but lacked a sense of direction. Their lives seemed strangely empty. Had the terrible sacrifices of the past years proved to be for nothing? Their labour for the construction and defence of the country had resulted only in the ignominy of occupation. The new Kampuchea in which so many had placed so much hope in April 1975 seemed no more than an ephemeral nightmare, past and gone. Where were they to go from here? people asked themselves.

Kylin Chi and Kim An, Bun's sister and brother-in-law, made their way back secretly to Phnom Penh to try to find out what had happened to the family house. They found it intact, and even recovered some silver hidden four years before. Bun and Phiny left Phum Andong in February, but only went as far as Muk Kampol district to the north of Phnom Penh. There Bun worked for two months in the district office before obtaining permission to enter the city in April to work for the new government of President Heng Samrin. Vietnamese forces occupying the city mounted guard at all important points   the Royal Palace, the museum, government ministries, and larger factories. In the first months of occupation, Vietnamese troops selectively looted the deserted city. Bun saw convoys of Vietnamese army trucks loaded with the spoils of war. Whatever was considered of value was collected into warehouses for transportation to Vietnam. Most went by truck or boat, but some valuable items were flown out. Some factories were even completely dismantled, presumably to obtain spare parts for use in similar factories in southern Vietnam. Heng Samrin forces were relegated to minor duties, such as population control.

The Vietnamese victory was the signal for yet another vast movement of people. Thousands, like Bun, began making for Phnom Penh, some to return home, others because they sought work and thought the capital the best place to find employment. Along the main roads Vietnamese soldiers gave lifts in army jeeps and trucks to all who could pay them in gold or jewellery.

Not everyone from Phnom Penh was allowed to return as no essential services were functioning. Vietnamese engineers and technicians were brought in to restore power and water supplies, but it proved a massive job after four years of neglect. People prevented from moving into the centre of the city were permitted to camp in the suburbs and surrounding countryside. Sometimes people were allowed to enter the city to scavenge for what they could find — as observed by foreign journalists and photographers who flew into Phnom Penh for the first time.

When Bun and Phiny eventually obtained permission to go into the centre of the city the destruction still evident was almost beyond belief. The gracious city they had left four years before with its wide boulevards and handsome villas, its pagodas and government buildings, was a sad and semi-deserted shadow of its former self. People were still not allowed to move freely back to their own homes. Only those attached to some arm of the new administration or its workforce had the right to live in the city, and only then in allotted accommodation in the immediate vicinity of their offices or worksites. Nearby mansions were reserved for ministers and heads of various services, and for Vietnamese experts assisting the new regime.

The new administration issued a call for all former intellectuals and technicians to report to the authorities in order to offer their services for the reconstruction of the country. Bun reported as instructed, and was assigned to the Ministry of Information and Propaganda, as an animator in the cinema section. Before taking up his position, however, he was required to attend a series of political seminars at which Kampuchean cadres of the Heng Samrin regime and their Vietnamese backers outlined and attempted to justify the new political line. Vietnamese "experts" lectured on Vietnam's policies towards Kampuchea, on

The spoils of victory.

Phnom Penh . . . amid the ruins.

Vietnamese-Kampuchean relations, and on the need for close co-operation between the three states of Indochina (including Laos). The Vietnamese tried hard to get their Kampuchean charges to acknowledge the spirit of altruism which alone was said to have motivated Vietnam to rid Kampuchea of the Khmer Rouge. All Kampucheans were urged to be grateful to the Vietnamese. Those who showed a proper attitude, conceded the need for close relations with Vietnam, and rejected the ultranationalism of the Khmer Rouge were sent for periods of three to six months for political training in Vietnam. When they returned they were appointed to senior positions within the administration under the supervision of Vietnamese cadres. Bun was promised he would be sent to East Germany to learn animation if he accepted the new order.

Disputes frequently occurred in the early months of 1979 between intellectuals and technicians who had been persecuted by the Khmer Rouge and returned to Phnom Penh and former Khmer Rouge cadres in the new regime (most of them from the Eastern Zone). But political debate was risky. The new political line was rigorously enforced and there was no room for democratic discussion on the future of the country. Those working for the new administration again had to write out their biographies, in which they confessed their previous errors — this time during the Pol Pot period. Later several hundred people were detained and sent for intensive re-education. Unlike re-education under the Khmer Rouge, however, the word meant what it said, and after the prescribed period detainees returned to Phnom Penh.

Political re-education emphasized the sufferings of the Kampuchean people under Pol Pot, the sadism and bestiality of the regime and the misery and terror of the population. From this, it was stressed, only the timely assistance of their Vietnamese brothers had rescued them. Only the arrival of the Vietnamese army had prevented the genocide of the Khmer people at the hands of the Khmer Rouge. To back up this line of argument, the Vietnamese encouraged the Heng Samrin regime to publicize the massacres committed by the Khmer Rouge. Mass graves were exhumed where hundreds, in places thousands, of bodies had been buried, many of them women and children, some with ropes still binding their hands behind their backs.

The prison of Tuol Sleng was opened to the public as a museum of horror to which all foreign visitors were taken. Parties of civil servants, soldiers, peasants and school children were brought to view the atrocities of the previous regime. Bun visited Tuol Sleng in June 1979, and was deeply shocked by the experience. He could not comprehend the enormity of such a regime or understand the warped mentality of those responsible for such crimes. The Kampuchean people must be told of the atrocities committed by Angkar on its own cadres. The whole world must know. Bun returned to his work at the Ministry of Information determined to play his part in publicizing the crimes of the Khmer Rouge. He brought the rest of his family to live in Phnom Penh. In July Phiny gave birth to their first child, a daughter whom they named Chankreusna.

But Bun was not happy with the new constraints under which he worked. He disliked the ubiquitous presence of the Vietnamese. In every ministry and office ultimate authority rested with the Vietnamese "experts" attached to it. Life was still very hard, and food supplies still meagre. Public servants received a monthly ration of 13 kilograms of rice and maize per person. Bun was also unhappy about other developments. A black market had sprung up, and bribery was commonplace. To get a job working in a government-run factory a man had to give the manager a third of a *damloeung* of gold. Payment was demanded to pass government checkpoints, to obtain interviews, to process documents. Official morality was lax. Because so many men had been killed, senior officials were in the habit of entering into polygamous relations with women who wanted only to obtain a roof over their heads and food for their children. The Minister of Information and Propaganda, Keo Chanda, was reported to be keeping five "wives" in different houses in Phnom Penh.[2]

But it was an experience at work which brought home to Bun the fact that personal liberty and freedom of expression were still severely limited. The incident seemed minor enough, but he knew it was one which would be held against him, and which would be entered in his biographical dossier. He was drawing cartoons for animated propaganda films lauding the benevolence and friendship of Vietnam in liberating Kampuchea from the Khmer Rouge. His drawings showed smiling Vietnamese troops merrily helping Kampuchean peasants, but they were not acceptable to the Vietnamese in charge of the work. Bun was accused of deliberately drawing some of the Vietnamese with protruding teeth and was asked to explain himself. Was he poking fun at the Vietnamese? Was he secretly in sympathy with the misguided policies, the radical nationalist racism of the former regime? The charge was a serious one. The whole section was assembled to criticize Bun's work and he was called upon to criticize himself. Abjectly he conceded his failure. Unconsciously

More propaganda.

he had let himself be influenced by the false propaganda of the Pol Pot clique. He had not shown in his drawings the proper respect and gratefulness which all Kampucheans felt towards their Vietnamese benefactors. He pledged to reform himself through political study, and was lucky enough to be let off a course of re-education. But it had been a close call. Bun decided to leave Kampuchea.

It was no longer difficult to leave the country. From Phnom Penh regular convoys of trucks took rice out to the provinces. For about half a *damloeung* of gold anybody, escapees, black marketeers, those still desperately seeking relatives and friends, could hitch a ride. No questions were asked, though additional bribes might be needed at checkpoints. The major highway to the Thai border was National Route Five via Kompong Chhnang, Pursat and Battambang to Sisophon and the frontier town of Poipet. The desperate need for even the most basic consumer goods led the authorities to turn a blind eye to the massive smuggling which went on from Thailand.

At the beginning of December 1979, Bun and his family took the last of their gold (which his mother had left hidden in their house in Phnom Penh and found again when she returned), to pay for their transport to Poipet. On the truck on which they rode, about forty people were lodged precariously atop bags of rice donated by international agencies to relieve the famine in Kampuchea. At more than fifty checkpoints Kampuchean soldiers searched the travellers and confiscated most of their remaining belongings. The road was in a terrible state but otherwise the trip was uneventful. On 19 December the Ung family crossed into Thailand where they were sent to the Khao-i-dang refugee camp. There they were accepted for resettlement in Australia, and the family arrived in Brisbane on 24 May 1980.

On his arrival Bun possessed only the clothes he stood up in, and an Australian twenty-cent piece given to him by a Vietnamese girl whom he met on the aircraft flying out. In Brisbane they were welcomed by Bun's elder brother Bun An. Miraculously all Bun's immediate family had survived an ordeal lasting almost four years from which few families emerged unscathed. All Bun's brothers and sisters were still alive, though more than forty of his near and distant relatives in Maesor Prachan were dead. Phiny had not been so lucky. She had lost her father, three brothers, two sisters and more than fifty other relatives.

Bun and his family left behind them a country whose future remained uncertain. In the Dangrek Ranges and the Cardamon mountains perhaps as many as 30,000 fanatically motivated

Khmer Rouge troops and cadres continued to hold out against Vietnamese occupation forces. For reasons of international politics which had nothing to do with humanitarian concern or the wishes of the majority of the Kampuchean people, the infamous and discredited leadership of the Khmer Rouge continued to enjoy majority international recognition and a seat in the United Nations as official representatives of their nation.

The agony of Kampuchea is not yet over. In July 1982 a Coalition Government of Democratic Kampuchea was formed between three mutually suspicious guerrilla organizations fighting the People's Republic of Kampuchea from bases along and across the Thai border. In addition to the numerically dominant Khmer Rouge, these organizations included a small force loyal to Prince Sihanouk, and a larger one led by former Kampuchean Prime Minister Son Sann. The coalition is recognized and supported by the People's Republic of China, and the group of nations comprising ASEAN (the Association of Southeast Asian Nations — Thailand, Malaysia, Indonesia, Singapore and the Philippines). Aid is also provided by the United States and a number of international agencies.

The coalition is dedicated to the expulsion of all Vietnamese forces from Kampuchea. But the Vietnamese are unlikely to withdraw so long as there remains any likelihood that the Khmer Rouge could return to power. The outlook, therefore, is for more fighting, with Vietnamese troops defending the People's Republic of Kampuchea against Democratic Kampuchea coalition guerrillas armed and supplied by China and ASEAN.[3]

Until this stalemate over Kampuchea is resolved, its long-suffering people will continue to suffer, and the peace and stability of Southeast Asia will remain threatened. At the very least, all parties to the dispute over Kampuchea owe it to the Kampuchean people to help them put the tragedy of their past behind them, and live in peace and prosperity in their own land.

Notes

Chapter 1

1. Kampuchea is the transliteration of Cambodia introduced by the government of Democratic Kampuchea after April 1975, and retained by the People's Republic of Kampuchea since the overthrow of the Pol Pot regime in January 1979.

2. Population figures for Kampuchea can be little more than informed guesses. The last census, by no means accurate, was carried out in 1962. The Khmer Rouge themselves used the round figure of four million for the total urban population in April 1975. The majority of these, however, were peasant farmers who had fled the fighting of the previous five years, especially the massive American bombing, and not bourgeois opponents of the regime.

3. Known by the initials of its name in French as GRUNK, a body under the nominal leadership of Sihanouk as President, comprising ministers representing the National United Front of Kampuchea (FUNK), which had been set up by the Communist Party of Kampuchea (CPK) as an anti-Lon Nol coalition of Sihanouk loyalists and leftist insurgents.

4. The failure of most Kampucheans to appreciate the nature of the Khmer Rouge regime prior to 1975 is perhaps surprising in view of the information which was at the time available. See, for example, the account by Ith Sarin in his *Regrets for the Khmer Soul* (in Cambodian, but discussed by Timothy Michael Carney in *Communist Party Power in Kampuchea (Cambodia): Documents and Discussion*, Cornell University Southeast Asia Program, Data Paper No. 106 (January 1977)). Also Ith Sarin, "Nine Months with the Maquis", translated by U.S. Embassy, Phnom Penh, May 1973 (also reprinted in Carney). Kennth M. Quinn's article "Political Change in Wartime: the Khmer Krahom Revolution in Southern Cambodia, 1970-1974", *U.S. Naval War College Review*, Spring 1976, pp. 3-31, also draws on material then available, mostly refugee reports gathered in Vietnam.

5. On the Lon Nol regime and its failings during 1973 and 1974, see Donald Kirk, "Cambodia 1973: Year of the 'Bomb Halt' ", *Asian Survey* 14 (1974), pp. 89-100; and "Cambodia 1974: Governments on Trial", *Asian Survey* 15 (1975), pp. 53-60. Also Malcolm Caldwell and Lek Tan, *Cambodia in the Southeast Asian War* (New York and London: Monthly Review Press, 1973), chapter 7.

6. For an account of the terrible effect of U.S. bombing in Kampuchea on young Khmer Rouge peasant soldiers, see William Shawcross, *Sideshow: Kissinger, Nixon and the Destruction of Cambodia* (New York: Simon and Shuster, 1979), especially pp. 297-9.

7. Accounts of the evacuation of Phnom Penh were written by journalists who remained in the city, and were evacuated with diplomatic personnel and other foreigners overland to Thailand about three weeks after the fall of Phnom Penh. Detailed descriptions can be found in Francois Ponchaud, *Cambodia Year Zero*, translated by Nancy Amphoux (Harmondsworth: Penguin, 1978); Bernard Hamel, *De Sang et de Larmes: La grande deportation du Cambodge* (Paris: Albin Michel, 1977); and Pin Yathay, *L'Utopie Meurtriere: un rescape du genocide cambodgien temoigne* (Paris: Editions Robert Laffont, 1980). For a more popularly written and less reliable account in English, see John Barron and Anthony Paul, *Murder of a Gentle Land* (New York: Reader's Digest Press, 1977).

8. Extensive evidence now exists of massacres carried out by the Khmer Rouge immediately following their victory. This includes evidence submitted at the "Trial for Genocide of the Pol Pot-Ieng Sary Clique" held in Phnom Penh in August 1979, and evidence collected from refugees and submitted to the United Nations Commission on Human Rights in Geneva. Accounts of massacres can be found in Ponchaud, *Cambodia Year Zero* (chapters 2, 3 and 4), and in Barron and Paul, *Murder of a Gentle Land* (chapter 3).

9. On reasons for the evacuation of Phnom Penh and other towns, see Ponchaud, *Cambodia Year Zero*, pp. 34-8. For arguments justifying the evacuation, see George

Hildebrand and Gareth Porter, *Cambodia: Starvation and Revolution* (New York and London: Monthly Review Press, 1976).

10. Pin Yathay, *L'Utopie Meutriere*, p. 105.

11. On the occupation of Phnom Penh by the Khmer Rouge, see Michael Vickery, *Cambodia: 1975-1982* (Sydney: George Allen & Unwin, 1984) pp. 72-75.

12. Estimates of the number of the number of dead as a result of the evacuation of Phnom Penh and the first wave of executions are based in part on figures calculated by Michael Vickery in "Democratic Kampuchea — CIA to the rescue", *Bulletin of Concerned Asian Scholars* 14, no. 4 (1982), pp. 45-54. See also the assessment by Carlyle A. Thayer, "New Evidence of Kampuchea", *Problems of Communism* XXX, no. 3 (1981), pp. 91-6; and for a pro-Khmer Rouge view, David Boggett, "Democratic Kampuchea and Human Rights: Correcting the Record", *Ampo* 11 (1979), pp. 13-18. Ben Kiernan places the number of dead during the evacuation at around 20,000 (personal communication). All such figures can be little more than educated guesses, and mine are no more than that. (This book was written before I had the opportunity to read Craig Etcheson's study entitled *The Rise and Demise of Democratic Kampuchea* [Boulder, Colorado, Westview Press, 1984].)

Chapter 2

1. The following account draws heavily upon Ben Kiernan, "Origins of Khmer Communism", in *Southeast Asian Studies 1981* (Singapore: Institute of Southeast Asian Studies/Heinemann, 1982), pp. 161-80. Other books and articles on the origins of the Kampuchean communist movement include: Francois Debre, *Cambodge: La revolution de la foret* (Paris: Flammarion, 1976); Ben Kiernan and Chantou Boua (eds), *Peasants and Politics in Kampuchea 1942-1981* (London: Zed Press, 1982); Wilfred Burchett, *The China-Cambodia-Vietnam Triangle* (Chicago: Vanguard Books, and London: Zed Press, 1981) (chapters 4 and 4); Caldwell and Tan, *Cambodia in the Southeast Asian War*; Stephen R. Heder, "Kampuchea's Armed Struggle: The Origins of an Independent Revoution", *Bulletin of Concerned Asian Scholars* II (1979), pp. 2-23; Pierre Rousset, "Cambodia: Background to the Revolution", *Journal of Contemporary Asia* 7 (1977), pp. 513-28; Ben Kiernan, "Conflict in the Kampuchean Communist Movement", *Journal of Contemporary Asia* 10 (1980), pp. 7-74; and Stephen R. Heder, "Kampuchea: From Pol Pot to Pen Sovan to the Villages", in Khien Theeravit and MacAlister Brown (eds), *Indochina and Problems of Security and Stability in Southeast Asia* (Bangkok: Chulalongkorn University Press, 1981), pp. 16-62.

2. In the same way, Chinese acceptance of the division of Vietnam into two separate states in the north and the south caused deep and permanent resentment among many Vietnamese communist leaders.

3. Perhaps as many as 1,000 KPRP members remained in Kampuchea, not all of them politically active. The Party structure consisted of the Phnom Penh committee, seventeen provincial committees, and a separate committee for the Northern Regroupees.

4. At this congress So Phim is reported to have stood against Pol Pot for the position of Secretary-General. He was defeated because of the overrepresentation both of the Phnom Penh committee, and of the returned students. Probably the most important differences between the veteran former Issaraks and the returned students concerned their attitudes towards Sihanouk and towards the developing conflict in Vietnam. The students argued for immediate political struggle against the Sihanouk government based on their analysis of the class structure of Kampuchean society (an analysis which W.E. Willmott has shown to be faulty in "Analytical Errors of the Kampuchean Communist Party", *Pacific Affairs* 54 (1981), pp. 209-27). The veterans were more inclined to value Sihanouk's neutrality as a weapon in the struggle against U.S. imperialism being waged in Vietnam.

5. Their flight made it virtually impossible to organize another congress, with the result that, as Kiernan puts it, "neither vote nor opinion was to remove them from party power after that. Led by urban-based intellectuals, the party began preparing for a peasant revolution" ("Origins of Khmer Communism", p. 178).

6. For the mounting opposition to Sihanouk in the late 1960s, see: Milton Osborne, *Before Kampuchea: Preludes to Tragedy* Sydney and London: Allen and Unwin, 1979), and the same author's "Regional Disunity in Cambodia", *Australian Outlook* 22 (1968), pp. 317-33; Michael Leifer, "Rebellion or Subversion in Cambodia?", *Current History* (1969), pp. 88-93 and 112-13; Ben Kiernan, *The Samlaut Rebellion and Its Aftermath: The Origins of Cambodia's Liberation Movement*, Working Papers nos 4 and 5 (Melbourne: Monash University Centre of Southeast Asian Studies, 1975); J.L.S. Girling, "The Resistance in Cambodia", *Asian Survey* 12 (1972), pp. 549-63; Donald Kirk, "Cambodia's Economic Crisis", *Asian Survey* 11 (1971), pp. 238-55; and Michael Vickery, "Looking Back at Cambodia", *Westerly* no. 4 (December 1976), pp. 14-28 (reprinted in Kiernan and Boua, *Peasants and Politics*).

7. For an English translation of the Black Paper, see *Black Paper: Facts and Evidences of the Acts of Aggression and Annexation of Vietnam against Kampuchea* (New York: Foreign Affairs of Democratic Kampuchea, September 1978). For a discussion of this document, see Serge Thion, "The Ingratitude of the Crocodiles: The 1978 Cambodian Black Paper", *Bulletin of Concerned Asian Scholars* 12 (1980), pp. 38-54.

8. Reference to an Indochina federation can be found in "The Manifesto and Platform of the Vietnam Lao Dong Party", supplement to *People's China* vol 3, no 9 (May 1951), p. 8; and is referred to in Carlyle Thayer, "The "Two-Lines" Conflict in the Khmer Revolution", in Malcolm Salon (ed.), *The Vietnam-Kampuchea-China Conflicts: Motivations, Background, Significance* (Canberra: Working Paper 1, Department of Political and Social Change, Australian National University, March 1979), pp. 20-8.

9. For an account of Lon Nol's coup against Sihanouk, see T.D. Allman, "Anatomy of a Coup" in Jonathan S. Grant *et al.* (eds), *Cambodia: The Widening War in Indochina* (New York: Washington Square Press, 1971), pp. 97-104.

10. For events following the 1970 coup, see: Ben Kiernan, "The 1970 Peasant Uprising in Kampuchea", *Journal of Cointemporary Asia* 9 (1979), pp. 310-24; Michael Leifer, "Peace and War in Cambodia", *Southeast Asia* 1 (1971), pp. 59-73; Donald Kirk, "Revolution and Political Violence in Cambodia 1970-1974" in Joseph J. Zasloff and MacAlister Brown (eds), *Communism in Indochina* (Lexington, Mass.: Lexington Books, 1975); also Quinn, "Political Change in Wartime . . ."

11. Shawcross, *Sideshow*, p. 297. So deep was the hatred felt by the young Khmer Rouge soldiers for the Khmer and U.S. air forces that when they arrived at Battambang airport they destroyed two T-28 fighter-bombers with their bare hands. See David P. Chandler, with Ben Kiernan and Muy Hong Lim, *The Early Phases of Liberation in Northwestern Cambodia: Conversations with Peang Sophi*, Working Paper no. 10 (Melbourne: Monash University, Centre of Southeast Asian Studies, 1976).

12. Shawcross, *Sideshow*, p. 299.

13. The summary of Khmer Rouge policies decided on immediately following the fall of Phnom Penh is taken from Ben Kiernan, "Wild Chickens, Farm Chickens, and Cormorants: Kampuchea's Eastern Zone under Pol Pot", which he kindly allowed me to consult in manuscript form. The list is given on MS p.42, and is attested to by Sin Song, former political commissar for Region 24. Keirnan's study has since been published in D. Chandler and B. Kiernan (eds), *Revolution and its Aftermath in Kampuchea: eight essays* (New Haven, Conn.: Yale University Southeast Asian Monographs No. 25, 1983).

Chapter 3

1. This chapter is based on the personal experiences of Bunheang Ung and his immediate family. Other authors have discussed Khmer Rouge policy toward the family. Cf Vickery, *Cambodia: 1975-1982*, pp. 174-178.

2. Pin Yathay also mentions the frequent rumours of Sihanouk's return (cf. the "five conditions" referred to in *L'Utopie Meurtriere*, p. 119).

Chapter 4

1. This account of the woman executed for adultery is taken from Pin Yathay, *L'Utopie Meurtriere*. It is also quoted in Burchett, *Triangle*, pp. 116-17.
2. The Constitution of Democratic Kampuchea was published in translation by the *Review of Socialist Law* 2 (1976), pp. 189-203. It is discussed by David B. Chandler, "The Constitution of Democratic Kampuchea (Cambodia): The Semantics of Revolutionary Change", *Pacific Affairs* 49 (1976), pp. 506-616.
3. For the composition of the government, see *Asia Year Book* 1977 and 1978 (Hong Kong: Far Eastern Economic Review).

Chapter 5

1. Michael Vickery points out that differences in the implementation of policies are evident even in the evacuation of Phnom Penh: Eastern Zone troops were far less brutal to the evacuees than were Northern Zone forces. For a general discussion of differences between Zones, see Vickery, "Democratic Kampuchea — Themes and Variations", in Chandler and Kiernan, *Revolution and its Aftermath in Kampuchea*. For documentation of differences Zone by Zone, see Vickery, *Cambodia: 1975-1982.The principal sources for this chapter, however, are the personal accounts of Pin Yathay, in L'Utopie Meurtriere*, and the accounts of refugees recorded in Ponchaud, *Year Zero*, Burchett, *Triangle*, and Kiernan and Boua, *Peasants and Politics*.
2. For a discussion of the administrative divisions in Democratic Kampuchea, see Vickery, *Cambodia: 1975-1982*.
3. Information from interviews conducted on 5 December 1982, in Sydney, with Sytha Leang, formerly an architect in Phnom Penh, and Kim Hany Hong, a midwife, both of whom underwent transportation to new villages.

Chapter 6

1. For the persecution of religion under the Khmer Rouge, see Ponchaud, *Year Zero*, also the submission by Vietnam on "Elimination of all forms of religious intolerance: the situation in Kampuchea" presented to the 34th session of the United Nations General Assembly. All this chapter is based on the experiences of Bunheang Ung.

Chapter 7

1. For the significance of the early elimination of Hou Youn, see Anthony Barnett, "Democratic Kampuchea: A Highly Centralized Dictatorship" in Chandler and Kiernan, *Revolution and its Aftermath in Kampuchea*. Barnett maintains that the whole thrust and purpose of policies pursued by the Party centre was the consolidation of absolute power in the hands of the Pol Pot group (pp. 214-15).
2. This chapter is almost entirely based on the research of Ben Kiernan, one of a small but dedicated group of scholars whose work has done most to reveal the internal politics of the Khmer Rouge and the history of events in Kampuchea between 1975 and 1979. For purges within the Party during 1975-77, see Kiernan, "Pol Pot and the Kampuchean Communist Movement", in Kiernan and Boua *Peasants and Politics*. For events in the Eastern Zone, see Kiernan, "Wild Chickens, Farm Chickens" in Chandler and Kiernan, *Revolution and its Aftermath in Kampuchea*. Also Vickery, *Cambodia: 1975-1982*.
3. Kiernan and Boua, *Peasants and Politics*, p. 302.

Chapter 8

1. This chapter is again based on the harrowing personal experiences of Bunheang Ung.
2. Pin Yathay gives examples of Khmer Rouge failure to make use of Western-trained professional engineers in *L'Utopie Meurtriere*. See also the interview with Nhem Heng in Kathleen Gough, "Interviews in Kampuchea", *Bulletin of Concerned Asian*

Scholars 14, no. 4 (1982), p. 61. Ben Kiernan notes that Western-trained engineers were employed in the Eastern Zone until 1976, but nowhere else in the country (personal communication).

3. The fate of So Phim is related by Ben Kiernan in "Wild Chickens, Farm Chickens . . ." p. 191.

4. Youths were attracted into the army by the promise of larger food rations, and by the fact that "they did not have to work, and could kill people". Interview with a peasant boy named Sat in Kiernan and Boua, *Peasants and Politics*, p. 335.

5. Sihanouk describes how his youthful guards amused themselves by torturing and killing animals in the Palace grounds. See Norodom Sihanouk, *War and Hope: The Case for Cambodia*, translated by Mary Feeney (New York: Pantheon Books, 1980), p. 29.

Chapter 9

1. There is no adequate study yet on the ideology of the Khmer Rouge, but Ponchaud has probably made as careful a study as anyone. See *Cambodia Year Zero*, and "Le Kampuchea Democratique: Une revolution radicale", *Mondes Asiatiques* no. 6 (1976), pp. 153-80. See also Kiernan, "Conflict in the Kampuchean Communist Movement"; Heder, "Kampuchea's Armed Struggle"; Justice M. van der Kroef, "Political Ideology in Democratic Kampuchea", *Orbis* 22 (1979), pp. 1002-32; Joseph J. Zasloff and MacAlister Brown, "The Passion of Kampuchea", *Problems of Communism* (Jan-Feb, 1979), pp. 28-44; Serge Thion, "The Cambodian Idea of Revolution", David P. Chandler, "Seeing Red: Perceptions of Cambodian History in Democratic Kampuchea", and Anthony Barnett, "Democratic Kampuchea: A Highly Centralized Dictatorship" all in Chandler and Kiernan, *Revolution and its Aftermath in Kampuchea*. A sympathetic account based on meagre early reports can be found in Mean Sangkum, "Democratic Kampuchea: An Updated View", in *Southeast Asian Affairs 1977* (Singapore: Institute of Southeast Asian Affairs/Heinemann, 1978), pp. 93-106. Robert Newman has tried to shed some light on the nature of the Kampuchean revolution by comparing it to the revolution in Vietnam. See: Robert S. Newman, *Brahmin and Mandarin: A Comparison of the Cambodian and Vietnamese Revolutions*, Working Paper no. 15 (Melbourne: Monash University Centre of Southeast Asian Studies, 1978). David Chandler has placed events in Kampuchea in historical perspective in David P. Chandler, "The Tragedy of Cambodian History", *Pacific Affairs* 52 (1979), pp. 410-19. And for a *cri du coeur* on Western failure to prevent what was happening, see Jean Lacourture, *Survive le peuple Cambodgien* (Paris: Seuil, 1978).

2. Ben Kiernan points out that the Thai destroyed the Mon state in the course of their southward migration (personal communication).

3. The question of relations with Vietnam is a complex one. See the *Black Paper*, and Vietnam's response in *Kampuchea Dossiers* nos 1 and 2 (Hanoi, 1978). See also various documents translated in *Journal of Contemporary Asia* 8 (1978) pp. 249-59, 399-425. For the historical background, see Milton Osborne, "Kampuchea and Vietnam: A Historical Perspective", *Pacific Community* 9 (1978), pp. 249-63, and Gareth Porter, "Vietnamese Communist Policy Towards Kampuchea 1930-1970" in Chandler and Kiernan, *Revolution and its Aftermath in Kampuchea*. For a discussion of the border issue, see Marian Kirsch Leighton, "Perspectives on the Vietnam-Cambodia Border Conflict", *Asian Survey* 18 (1978), pp. 448-57; also Stephen R. Heder, "Origins of the Conflict" *Southeast Asia Chronicle*, No. 64 (1978); and by the same author, "The Kampuchean-Vietnamese Conflict", in David W.P. Elliott (ed.), *The Third Indochina Conflict* (Boulder Colorado: Westview Press, 1981), pp. 21-68. Relations between the two states are discussed, from a pro-Vietnamese point of view, by Wilfred Burchett in *The China-Cambodia-Vietnam Triangle*. See also Ben Kiernan, "Vietnam and the Governments and People of Kampuchea", *Bulletin of Concerned Asian Scholars* 11 (1979), pp. 19-25.

4. Sihanouk discusses Kampuchean-Vietnamese relations in Norodom Sihanouk, *Chroniques de guerre . . . et d'espoir* (Paris: Hachette Stock, 1979).

5. For a discussion on the effect of militarization on democratic processes and political mobilization, see Serge Thion, "The Cambodian Idea of Revolution", p. 27.

6. For these economic arguments, see the chapters by Hou Yuon and Hu Nim in Kiernan and Boua, *Peasants and Politics*. Also Khieu Samphan, *Cambodia's Economic and Industrial Development*, translated by Laura Summers, Cornell University Southeast Asia Program, Data Paper no. 111 (March 1979). And for a critique of these social analyses, see Willmott, "Analytical Errors of the Kampuchean Communist Party".

7. Serge Thion makes the interesting suggestion in "The Cambodian Idea of Revolution" (p. 28) that this "concept of linear loyalties linking people upward to a leader" harks back to the traditional Kampuchean concept of patronage and client loyalty (komlang).

8. The description of Tuol Sleng prison and discussion of Hu Nim's confession is taken from Chantou Boua, Ben Kiernan and Anthony Barnett, "The Bureaucracy of Death: Documents from Inside Pol Pot's Torture Machine", *New Statesman* 2 May 1980, pp. 669-76. The words of Democratic Kampuchea's national anthem are taken from the magazine *Democratic Kampuchea is Moving Forward* (August 1977), p. 2. Serge Thion has drawn attention to the Khmer Rouge obsession with blood in "The Cambodian Idea of Revolution" p. 31.

Chapter 10

1. The rights and wrongs of the Vietnamese-backed invasion of Kampuchea have been debated in the pages of journals such as the *Bulletin of Concerned Asian Scholars* and *Ampo*. The best week to week coverage is provided by the *Far Eastern Economic Review*.

2. For the situation in Kampuchea since the Vietnamese occupation, see the many reports by Nayan Chanda in the *Far Eastern Economic Review*. Also Stephen R. Heder, "Kampuchea 1980: Anatomy of a Crisis", *Southeast Asia Chronicle* no. 77 (1981), pp. 3-11; and Joseph J. Zasloff, "Kampuchea: A Question of Survival. Part 1: The Vietnamese Invasion and Its Aftermath. Part II: The Political Dimensions", *American Universities Field Staff Reports* nos 46 and 47 (1980). See also Heder, "Kampuchea: From Pol Pot to Pen Sovan to the Villages". Also Vickery, *Cambodia: 1975-1982*, Chapter 4.

3. On the continuing struggle for power in Kampuchea, see Roger Kershaw, "The Cambodian Non-Communist Opposition in the Present Impasse: A Diagnosis and a Proposal", *Asian Profile* 9 (1981), pp. 509-26; Dennis Duncanson, "Who will govern Cambodia?", *The World Today* 38 (1981), pp. 239-45; also Michael Leifer, "The Balance of Advantage in Indochina", *The World Today* 38 (1982), pp. 232-8. On the wider implications of the continuing conflict, see Justis M. van der Kroef, *Kampuchea: The Endless Tug of War*, School of Law, University of Maryland, Occasional Papers/Reprints Series on Contemporary Asian Studies no. 47 (1982); and also by the same author, "The Cambodian Conflict in Southeast Asia's Strategic Considerations", *Asian Profile* 8 (1980), pp. 181-96. For a suggested diplomatic solution to the Kampuchean problem, see Martin Stuart-Fox, "Resolving the Kampuchean Problem: The Case for an Alternative Regional Initiative", *Contemporary Southeast Asia* 4 (1982), pp. 210-25.

Index

EPILOGUE

Though the First Edition of this book was published in 1985, the story ended in July 1982 with the formation of the Coalition Government of Democratic Kampuchea (CGDK), which brought together in uneasy alliance of both the Khmer Rouge and two anti-communist guerrilla forces led by Prince Sihanouk (the United Front for an Independent, Neutral, Peaceful and Cooperative Cambodia, known by its French acronym as FUNCINPEC) and former prime minister Son Sann (the Khmer People's National Liberation Front, or KPNLF). It was an alliance of opportunity dedicated to one goal - overthrow of the Vietnamese-backed regime in Phnom Penh, the People's Republic of Kampuchea (PRK), and the expulsion of all Vietnamese from Cambodian soil. Of the three parties in the CGDK, the Khmer Rouge was the strongest militarily, had the most impregnable bases, and benefitted from unstinting Chinese support in the form of weapons and equipment supplied via Thailand. Assistance for the forces of Sihanouk and Son Sann came from ASEAN, notably Thailand and Singapore, and from the United States and other Western countries, including France and Australia. The PRK, by contrast, drew its support from Vietnam and the Soviet Union. The lines were thus drawn for the long and bitter military confrontation that lasted throughout the 1980s.

From its inception in 1979, the PRK set about, under Vietnamese direction, the momentous task of reconstructing the Cambodian state after the depredations of the Khmer Rouge. Order was restored, people resettled, cities and towns rebuilt. Only food aid provided by Vietnam and the Soviet Bloc prevented massive starvation. The PRK itself was a motley coalition made up of former pro-Vietnamese communists and Sihanoukists who had fled Cambodia even before the Khmer Rouge seized power, and former Khmer Rouge, mainly from the Eastern Zone, who had later sought asylum in Vietnam. The three most prominent leaders were Heng Samrin, a former Khmer Rouge division commander, Hun Sen, one of his regimental commanders, and Pen Sovan, a Vietnamese-trained cadre later purged as Secretary-General of the Kampuchean People's Revolutionary Party. Of the three, it was the young and wily Hun Sen who eventually assumed the mantle of leadership of the PRK.

Through the early 1980s the Vietnamese sought to achieve three things in Cambodia: to eliminate the rabidly anti-Vietnamese Khmer Rouge as a military and political force; to establish the PRK regime as the legitimate government of Cambodia; and to draw Cambodia firmly into a Vietnamese dominated *de facto* Indochina alliance (of which Laos was already a member). None, however, was successful. Khmer Rouge guerrilla forces were able to resist annual offensives to destroy them by retreating deep into their mountain redoubts, while the non-communist guerrilla forces took sanctuary across the Thai border. The PRK, while it gained some legitimacy internally from claiming to have freed the country from the Khmer Rouge, by condemning Pol Pot and Ieng Sary to death in absentia on the charge of genocide, and by permitting a revival of Buddhism, was never accorded the international recognition it arguably deserved. (Klintworth, 1989). Throughout this period, Cambodia's seat in the United Nations General Assembly was occupied by the CGDK. And while the PRK joined Vietnam and Laos in a common diplomatic front and cooperated closely with them in every way, this was never enough to destroy deep-seated suspicions over long-term Vietnamese intentions. When in the late 1980s the balance of forces began to change, even those Cambodians most beholden to Vietnam were prepared to put some distance between themselves and their Vietnamese mentors.

By the middle of the decade it was clear that the situation in Cambodia had reached a stalemate. Even with strong Vietnamese military support the PRK was unable to destroy the Khmer Rouge, as international support for Thailand precluded any attack on guerrilla sanctuaries inside Thai territory. On the other hand, no amount of guerrilla activity was going to be enough to overthrow the government in Phnom Penh. What it was doing, however, was make the cost of supporting the PRK and of keeping substantial forces in Cambodia an ever heavier burden for Vietnam - and for the Soviet Union. A United States orchestrated aid embargo not only deprived Vietnam of all non-communist bilateral economic assistance, but also loans from the principal multilateral aid donors, such as the World Bank and the Asian Development Bank. The Vietnamese economy was suffering, and Vietnam was falling ever further behind its Asian neighbours in the race for economic development. Yet resumption of much needed aid depended on withdrawal of Vietnamese troops from Cambodia. Chinese threats, meanwhile, to teach Vietnam a second "lesson" forced Hanoi to maintain a large army at combat readiness in the north; and the Vietnamese were left in no doubt that normalization of relations with China would be impossible while Vietnamese forces remained in Cambodia. As for the Soviet Union, it too wanted to cut its losses. Aid to Vietnam was costly, and the Chinese had let it be known that rapprochement between Moscow and Beijing also depended on withdrawal of Vietnamese forces from Cambodia. When the Soviet Union took the hard decision to withdraw its forces from Afghanistan, Moscow too began to urge Vietnam to withdraw from Cambodia.

In the face of such concerted pressure Vietnam was forced to reassess its options - but so too was the West where there was growing concern over the future power of a resuscitated Khmer Rouge. It was one thing to oppose the Vietnamese-backed PRK; it was quite another to replace it by a coalition in which the Khmer Rouge was quite evidently the most powerful and ruthless partner. Britain, followed by Australia, decided to withdraw recognition from the CGDK as part of a more balanced approach to the two sides. As the possibility of some form of accommodation increased, Vietnam announced that it would withdraw all its forces from Cambodia by the end of 1989. Despite some doubt over whether Hanoi really meant what it said, a window of opportunity opened up which some at least were determined to exploit. While the Cambodian factions themselves remained deeply antagonistic, it was left to outside powers to take the lead. Though China, the United States, and Thailand maintained their opposition to Hanoi and the PRK, other countries, notably Australia, Indonesia and France began searching for some resolution to the conflict.

After much diplomatic activity in several of the world's capitals, an international conference was held in Paris in August 1989, jointly convened by France and Indonesia. Present in addition to the four Cambodian factions were Vietnam and Laos, the five permanent members of the Security Council (the USA, USSR, Britain, France and China, usually referred to thereafter as the Perm Five), the remaining five members of ASEAN, Japan, Canada, India, Australia and the Secretary General of the United Nations. Not surprisingly, this unwieldy group failed to bring about immediate settlement of the conflict, though it did focus attention on some of the key issued to be addressed.

A simultaneous initiative was the series of Joint Informal Meetings (JIM), held in Jakarta under Indonesian auspices, which attempted to find common ground between the four Cambodian factions. But no breakthrough occurred. A concurrent series of meetings between Prince Sihanouk and Hun Sen was equally unproductive. An even less successful attempt to broker a settlement came when Japan and Thailand co-hosted a meeting of the Cambodian factions in Tokyo in June 1990. Though scheduled to last two days, this broke up after 25 minutes over disagreement on the permissible size of Khmer Rouge delegation.

More successful was an Australian proposal that the United Nations should play a leading role in bringing about a solution to the Cambodian conflict. Australian Foreign Minister Gareth Evans gained American backing for his plan for a UN supervised cease-fire to be followed by a UN administered transition period leading up to free and fair elections. A UN agency would be established to be responsible for verifying that all Vietnamese forces had left the country (the Khmer Rouge claimed many remained), enforcing the cease-fire, and organizing the elections. This Australian plan was taken up at meetings of the Perm 5 on Cambodia beginning in January 1990. Though China had been cool to the plan at first, agreement was reached that, since the Cambodian factions themselves were hopelessly divided, the UN would have to play a significant role in any peace process.

By the end of the fifth Perm Five meeting in July 1990, the key elements of the Australian plan had been adopted. A Supreme National Council would be established in Cambodia (the exact composition of which was left open) to represent the sovereign state of Cambodia. This would then delegate power to a UN Transitional Authority in Cambodia (UNTAC), which in turn would ensure that all foreign troops had withdrawn, that all outside military assistance had ceased, and that a general cease-fire was being observed. When these conditions were fulfilled, an election would be held.

Chinese agreement had been crucial in arriving at this solution, particularly in pressuring the Khmer Rouge to accept it. In return, however, the Khmer Rouge were determined to be included on an equal footing with the other factions in the Supreme National Council. To this the PRK, now renamed the State of Cambodia (SOC), objected, as did Vietnam. The SOC, as the regime in power in Phnom Penh, also objected to handing over its authority to UNTAC, preferring instead to organize the election itself under UN supervision. A new deadlock thereupon ensued, lasting into early 1991.

The rapidly changing balance of international forces as the Soviet Union, on the verge of collapse, sought new accommodations with the West and China weakened Vietnamese support for the SOC. Reluctantly, the authorities in Phnom Penh agreed to the Perm Five formula. At the same time, a new military government in Thailand brought pressure to bear on the Khmer Rouge. Agreement was reached that Prince Sihanouk should be Chairman of the Supreme National Council (SNC), on which the SOC (with six members) had equal representation with the CGDK (renamed the National Government of Cambodia), which had two members each from FUNCINPEC, the KPNLF, and the Khmer Rouge. On 1 May 1991, all four factions accepted a cease-fire. More negotiations followed, in Indonesia, Pattaya (Thailand) and Beijing. Finally, on 23 October, eighteen nations meeting in Paris signed the treaty that ended thirteen years of war in Cambodia. Prince Sihanouk, duly reinstated as head of state (the *coup* that ousted him in 1970 was declared illegal), returned in triumph to Phnom Penh on 14 November. Leaders of the KPNLF (Son Sann) and the Khmer Rouge (Khieu Samphan) flew in a few days later, along with advance UN personnel.

It took almost a year for all UNTAC contingents to arrive in Cambodia. By October 1992, some 2,500 civilian administrators, 3,500 civilian police, and 16,000 military peacekeepers had been deployed under the overall direction of Yasushi Akashi, an experienced Japanese diplomat. Military personnel were under the command of Australian Lieutenant-General

John Sanderson. Their role was to oversee the voluntary demobilization of 70 per cent of the military forces of the four factions assembled in cantonment areas, followed by the remaining 30 per cent prior to national elections scheduled for May 1993. They were also to verify that all foreign (that is, Vietnamese) forces had withdrawn from Cambodia, and that no new ones entered the country. Meanwhile mines were to be cleared, security established, and all those Cambodians eligible to vote (up to five million) entered on electoral roles.

Almost immediately, however, the peace plan ran into intransigent opposition from the Khmer Rouge. Khmer Rouge troops failed to present themselves at designated re-groupment areas, on the grounds that not all Vietnamese forces had left Cambodia. Moreover the Khmer Rouge violated the cease-fire, murdered Vietnamese civilians (up to one million Vietnamese who previously had lived in Cambodia had returned since 1979), and refused to cooperate with UNTAC. They also objected to continued SOC control over key ministries and most local administration. Even Chinese pressure was to no avail. UN anger took the form of a resolution demanding Khmer Rouge cooperation, but on the ground UNTAC forces were reluctant to engage the Khmer Rouge.

Yet despite the failure of UNTAC to disarm the factions, and in the face of Khmer Rouge recalcitrance and SOC intimidation, the UN went ahead with organizing elections. Cambodians both in the country and abroad were registered (with the exception of those under Khmer Rouge control); twenty political parties were able to mount electoral campaigns; and all Cambodians were informed of their rights as citizens and voters (through UNTAC's popular radio station and by travelling groups of actors and informants). Meanwhile, UNTAC also pushed ahead with its massive program to resettle some 365,000 Cambodian refugees from camps inside the Thai border.

Fears that the Khmer Rouge would disrupt the elections did not in the end materialize, though just why was unclear. The KR leadership may have been divided in its response, or have misjudged the likely result (believing Sihanouk's popularity would win a landslide for FUNCINPEC). In any event, the election went ahead over a six-day period (23-28 May) with remarkably few incidents and with just on 90 per cent voter participation. This was a turnout beyond even the most optimistic expectations, a remarkable expression of the hope of common Cambodians that the bloodshed and trauma of the previous years could be put behind them, and of their confidence in the fairness and freedom of the electoral process.

The outcome of the elections were more or less as expected. FUNCINPEC won 45.47 per cent of the vote, polling particularly well in the urban areas, and thereby gaining 58 of the 120 seats in the Constituent (subsequently the National) Assembly. The SOC's Cambodian People's

Party (CPP) won 38.23 per cent, doing better in the rural areas and receiving 51 seats. The KPNLF's Buddhist Liberal Democratic Party with ten seats, and the Moulinaka party with one, were the only two other parties with sufficient votes to be represented in parliament. These results were a disappointment for the CPP, but a severe blow for the Khmer Rouge which found itself reviled and marginalized.

The Assembly met for the first time on 14 June 1993, and twelve days later the two major parties agreed on formation of a Provisional National Government of Cambodia (PNGC) with their leaders, Prince Norodom Ranariddh and Hun Sen, as first and second prime ministers respectively. A new constitution was adopted on 21 September establishing Cambodia as a constitutional monarchy with Sihanouk as King. This in turn cleared the way for the establishment of a new coalition Royal Government of Cambodia, which completed part at least of the task for which UNTAC had been set up - at a cost of some US$2 billion. What had not been achieved was disarmament of the Khmer Rouge or their inclusion in the political life of the country.

All attempts to reach a compromise with the Khmer Rouge were rebuffed, and after fighting broke out in the west of the country, the National Assembly passed a law declaring the Khmer Rouge an illegal organization. The Khmer Rouge retaliated by kidnapping and murdering several foreign hostages. Tourism declined, drought wrecked the eastern provinces, and only a substantial international aid program kept the fledgling government financially afloat. Nor was the coalition a comfortable one. Even as early as 1994, Hun Sen was already emerging as the more powerful of the two prime ministers, while divisions were increasingly evident in FUNCINPEC. Towards the end of the year, Prince Ranariddh dismissed his internationally respected finance minister, Sam Rainsy, an action which also precipitated the resignation of his half-brother Prince Norodom Sirivudh as Minister of Foreign Affairs. Both had spoken out in favour of human rights and press freedom.

But FUNCINPEC was not the only party to experience fissiparous pressures under the impact of changed political and economic forces in Cambodia. Son Sann was ousted as leader of the BLDP, and the party's political declined even further. As corruption became more blatant, and human rights violations increased, so too did political conflict as both the principal parties resorted to bribery and coercion to strengthen their hands. Perhaps the only bright point was continued international support in the form of the International Committee for the Reconstruction of Cambodia, a body established to coordinate economic aid and other assistance. Meanwhile the economy stagnated as a result of poor direction and massive smuggling.

Yet for the next two years, through a combination of internal politicking and external pressure (King Sihanouk's cancer unfortunately weakened the influence of the throne), the coalition government managed to hold together. Sam Rainsy formed a new opposition party which immediately became the target for Hun Sen's security forces, while Sirivudh was exiled on a charge of plotting to assassinate the second prime minister. But the real danger came from the gradually disintegrating Khmer Rouge. While military attempts to eliminate the Khmer Rouge met with little success, a series of defections in 1996 accomplished what the Royal Cambodian Armed Forces could not. After months of negotiations, Ieng Sary brought two divisions of Khmer Rouge troops over to the government side. Others followed, leaving the remaining "hard-line" leadership in disarray. Differences over how to respond to offers of amnesty and political alliance from FUNCINPEC negotiators led in 1997 to the execution of Khmer Rouge "minister of defence" Son Sen and his family. Thereupon what was left of the Khmer Rouge (led by Khien Samphan) turned on their erstwhile leader and arrested and condemned Pol Pot, not to death as he deserved, but to life imprisonment in a jungle hideaway.

The disintegration of the Khmer Rouge proved, however, to be the catalyst that brought about the collapse of the coalition government. In a lightning *coup* in July 1997 Hun Sen's forces destroyed Ranariddh's security apparatus, several leaders of which were brutally assassinated. Ranariddh himself fled the country, though several senior FUNCINPEC officials remained. The trigger for Hun Sen's move seems to have been CPP fear that a political alliance between FUNCINPEC and the Khmer Rouge would tip the balance against it in the general elections scheduled for 1998. The ASEAN states signalled their displeasure by deferring Cambodia's admission to the organization when Burma and Laos joined, but there was otherwise little foreign powers could do. FUNCINPEC's Ung Huot was subsequently sworn in as first prime minister in place of Ranariddh, but power lay firmly in the hands of Hun Sen.

So by the end of 1997, the fate of Cambodia hung once again in the balance, with the possibility of renewed fighting and political instability. For the leaders of the country, division and distrust, the legacy of the Pol Pot years, ran too deep to be overcome - even for the national good. For the people too, their agony continued. The task of rebuilding Cambodia still lies ahead, but it will take years to accomplish, for the spectre of the murderous revolution will not easily be exorcised.

Hospital patients set to work during convalescence.